LIFE AND LOVE

by Ray Garfield

Dedication

Special thanks to my friend Sally, who encouraged me to write this book and to Laura, my wife of 42 years, for her loving support and cooperation along the way.

© 1983 Ray Garfield

All rights reserved

Published by Ray Garfield
P.O. Box 4125
Clearlake, California 95422

Production Assistance:
Whatever Publishing, Inc.
P.O. Box 137
Mill Valley, California 94941

Cover design by Kathleen Vande Kieft

ISBN 0-9609856-0-3

Contents

PART ONE: The Nature and Purpose of Life

1 **Our Physical Environment**   13
   Construction of matter at the molecular level; how vastly different it is from the way we see it; even the most solid-appearing matter is mostly empty space; how matter is precipitated from the ether.

2 **Edgar Cayce and Reincarnation**   21
   Cayce's life and work, and the many references to reincarnation in his thousands of readings.

3 **The Mechanics of Reincarnation**   27
   Our four bodies; the seven planes of existence; nutation; how, when and why souls or Egos reincarnate; the four great civilizations on our planet; the Astral Plane, heaven and hell.

4 **Karma**   33
   What it is, and how it works; its function as part of the Natural Law of the Universe; reincarnating to improve karmic balance.

5 **The Brotherhoods**   41
   History and development of Their organization, activities and achievements; degrees of advancement; their philosophy on sex.

6 **The Bible**   47
   Its interpretation by the churches; changes in meaning through translation; biblical prophesies; Armageddon and the Great Cataclysm.

7 **Immorality in the Business World**   55
   Sharp practices, unfair competition and manipulation of government; little-known events in communist

Russia and Hitler's Germany; multinational organizations, cartels and megabankers; the Council on Foreign Relations and the Round Table.

8 **Creation**   **61**
Precipitation of matter from the ether by Mind; how the universe was created, step by step; man's development, and his eventual endowment with Mind; the urgency of man's advancement because of the short time remaining to him on the physical plane.

9 **Doomsday**   **67**
Geological and astronomical events leading up to the cataclysm, with Armageddon preceding it, and the utter destruction to follow.

10 **The Important Things in Life**   **73**
The Black Mentalists and their effect on our lives; how to circumvent them; man's freedom of choice to turn toward good or evil; definition of sin; effect of tobacco, alcohol and drugs on the body; physiological effects of emotional stress; learning to control your environment by raising the level of your thoughts; sex in your life.

11 **Life on the Astral Plane**   **81**
Its purpose; various levels of existence; auras and sympathetic vibrations; their relationship to the quality of one's thoughts; elevating the level of your thoughts now will insure a better Astral life.

12 **A Sound Body and Mind**   **87**
Some tips for longevity; the value of sunlight; the dangers and benefits of Hatha yoga as a means of bodybuilding.

13 **Clairvoyance**   **93**
Rajah yoga, The Brotherhoods' way; interference from Black Mentalists with attempts to contact the Astral Plane; overcoming the barrier between the conscious and the subconscious through greater awareness; yoga among primitive tribes; faith and the body; the Twelve Great Virtues.

PART TWO: The Power of Love

14 How The Brain Develops   **101**
Interlocking of the mind and brain; importance of a cheerful, positive mental outlook on one's well-being; the brain's physiological and evolutionary step-by-step growth; necessity for early training and exposure to the environment; a return to the family concept needed; the Early Learning school at Stelle, Illinois.

15 Mind — Where Love Begins   **107**
The Mind often goes "out of body" during sleep; the ten qualities of Mind; effect of the media on Mind; logic vs. emotions; Love, the most powerful emotion; thought waves from Mind propagated through the ether; how thought impulses are recorded in the brain; the need for selectivity in accepting thoughts; why one should think of everything as being good.

16 Achieving Happiness   **113**
The story of James A. Garfield; intelligence is everywhere; summary of topics covered so far.

17 What is Love?   **119**
Loving takes practice; the soul needs exercise, the same as the body does; we learn love by being involved in the mainstream of life; love must be initiated by thought; material things do not last, but love is eternal, for God is Love.

18 The Lower Centers of Consciousness   **125**
Early man's reaction of "fight or flight" still persists; the brain must be deprogrammed of this notion before progress can be made to convert one's addictions into preferences, and thus rise above the lower levels of security, sensation and power.

19 The Love Center of Consciousness   **131**
Learning to Love unconditionally requires practice; twelve pathways to higher consciousness.

20 **Extending the Love Center**   **139**
A thumbnail description of the seven centers of consciousness; your addictions are not your real self, and should be discarded; you need not change your way of living, just your mental attitude; you find that people are friendly, and your horizons expand; and your love for others brings more happiness for you.

21 **Aids to Attaining Your Goal**   **147**
The sixth and seventh centers of consciousness help you to become aware of your true self, and to view the dramas of life from a detached viewpoint, freeing you from the whims of your subconscious addictions; five ways to change your addictions into preferences.

22 **Be Master of Yourself**   **155**
The concept of "self" as an entity, and as an activity; clearing the Mind of barriers to its efficient operation; complexity of the brain's thought processes; why thought impulses are not true to the facts; thought-processing systems in the brain; an interview with Will Durant.

23 **Practicing the Virtues**   **163**
A description of each of the virtues.

24 **Selecting a Suitable Environment**   **169**
Getting away from the distractions of the cities.

25 **What is Reality?**   **175**
The many types of reality besides our own environment; reality is different to different people; quotations from famous thinkers of all eras; the philosophy of the Brotherhoods stands up where all others fail.

26 **Learning to Love**   **179**
Children can teach us about love, if we try to understand them; when anger flares up, love goes out the window; open your heart and let the love flow out — and in.

Preface

Our society is sick from fear and personal alienation while political and religious figures exploit the growing rage and divisiveness. The effective antidotes are truth and love, and Ray Garfield's *Life and Love* reiterates the Path by which a human being can achieve freedom from fear. The truths Mr. Garfield places before us are ages old and have been proferred to mankind by every great philosopher; however, mankind has rarely heeded this invitation to greater serenity, security, and spiritual uplift. *Life and Love* says it clearly and concisely for our times. Perhaps the personal turmoil so many people are experiencing today is the needed incentive to hear and apply these simple universal principles. They can fill our society's desperate need to form a loving network between all mankind and help us rediscover the sacred gratifications thus received by every participant.

Eklal Kueshana
(Richard Kieninger)

Foreword

The basic idea behind this book is to bring together into one volume the more important elements of the Philosophy of The Brotherhoods, an organization of scientist-philosophers dedicated to improving and preserving the best of civilization, and information from the book *Handbook to Higher Consciousness*, by Ken Keyes, Jr., Ken Keyes Center, 790 Commercial Avenue, Coos Bay, Oregon 97420. The source for the information about The Brotherhoods is *The Ultimate Frontier* by Eklal Kueshana, published by The Stelle Group, Stelle, Illinois 60919. Additional material comes from various other sources, which are acknowledged in the text. It is hoped that your interest will be sparked in reading this book, so that you will follow it up by reading the two mentioned above.

We hope this book will help you, the reader, to find a more fulfilling life, true happiness and spiritual advancement through a better understanding of our world, and through learning to love one another and thus find the inner peace we are all seeking.

PART ONE
The Nature and Purpose of Life

Chapter One
Our Physical Environment

After I retired from business a few years ago, I began to turn my attention away from chasing the almighty dollar to more philosophical thoughts, such as the reason for our being on this earth, and what life is all about. Where did man come from, and where is he going? Is there a supreme force of some kind that runs the universe? These are questions that man has asked for countless generations, and he is still floundering and wondering about it all, without much success in finding answers. Believe it or not, this book will answer most of these questions to your satisfaction, or at least give you a solid basis for forming your opinions. Where do I get this priceless information? That is part of the story — a true story — that has been available in print for a good many years, but which is still not very well known to the general public. This is "strong stuff" — as one reader described it — and not everyone will accept it, or some may dismiss it without becoming involved with it. But it is my hope that some will see it as the only logical explanation of the phenomena of the universe, and will embrace it and profit thereby, not only for themselves, but for the whole world they live in.

Let us take a look around us, and try to perceive the people in our world from an unbiased and detached viewpoint.

We find a great many people completely engrossed in their material world, bent on making money, pursuing pleasure, manipulating others to achieve their power goals, and in general competing against each other instead of lovingly helping one another for mutual "Egoic" development — that is, full development of our mind and soul. I believe all men and women need to live spiritually as well as materially in order to achieve real happiness and inner peace. This is a lesson that too many of us have not yet learned. We all have a conscience which tells us when things are right and when they are wrong, when we are good and when we are bad, if we will but use it rather than reject it. As we shall see later, our every thought and action is a potent force that is multiplied and amplified by repetition, somewhat like a radio signal going through a receiver. If they are positive in nature, they can help you and those in contact with you to attain a happier life. If they are negative, they can do just the reverse.

Going back to our overall view of today's world, now let us consider material things. We spend our lives collecting them, and we no doubt enjoy them for a while, but is this the primary goal we should strive for, as in the "American Dream"? I don't think so. All these objects we collect are only temporary, and I am thinking of more permanent values.

Besides having a conscience, man has been endowed with another faculty called intuition. This power is not used by us nearly as much as it could be, with training. Because of it, man feels a bond between himself and God, between himself and nature. Have you ever felt this bond, when standing in the solitude of the great redwood forests, or standing on a bluff overlooking the ocean, watching the endless parade of waves and breakers, or watching the magnificent splash of color in a sunset? Man intuitively worships these things, the wonders of nature, because they are part of God's plan for our enjoyment and advancement.

Religion has taken many forms through the ages, and it has been divided and corrupted until it is no longer recognizable as the expression of the simple laws of the universe with which man began his existence. Those of the

Christian faith today believe in it because it has been handed down to them from generation to generation, not because they have analyzed it and found it to be satisfactory to them. As science and technology advance, some find it more and more difficult to accept the teachings of present-day religion. We are finding that our five senses do not perceive the real world, but only a small part of it. Even with such marvelous technical advances as the electron microscope, we extend our perception only a little further, leaving a vast amount of knowledge still beyond our grasp.

What about death, heaven and hell? These are also questions that have been unanswered, although the churches have given us answers which many cannot accept. I have a better explanation, one that will remove the fear of death, and which discards the concept of eternal hell-fire and damnation.

Since man is beginning to find out just how much he doesn't know about the universe, many scientists and philosophers are becoming more open-minded about the possibility of ESP, clairvoyance and other qualities of the mind which cannot be proven as a mathematical certainty. ESP and clairvoyance are being used by law enforcement officers to solve crimes, sometimes with astounding results. Many instances of this kind have been reported in the press. Governments are investigating ESP and other occult powers as an addition to their war machines. The Soviet Union is in the forefront in these experiments. And there are many other instances where the occult has been in evidence, and it can no longer be totally discounted. So we must assume that here again we have found a phenomenon that our five senses cannot perceive, but which nevertheless does exist. As we train our minds to a state of higher consciousness, we shall see that these occult powers will come naturally to us, so that occult manifestations can not only be perceived by us, but also controlled.

But it will come naturally, not by forcing it as in the practice of certain forms of Yoga. First, we must attain a state of higher consciousness, and that involves learning to love everyone — unconditionally. This was one of Christ's admonitions: "love thy neighbor as thyself."

It is necessary before going on with other subjects, to spend a few minutes discussing our world and our universe, in order to understand what follows. We know that all things are made up of atoms, which in turn combine to form molecules of the various substances which we call matter, and these substances can be either solid, liquid or gaseous. These elements and compounds of elements are what make up our world and the entire universe, as far as science has been able to determine. Moon rock samples contain the same elements as those found here on earth, and samples of martian soil indicate the same thing. By analyzing the light coming from our sun and from other stars, we find that they also are made of the same elements, but not in the same proportions. Going back down to the other end of the scale, we find that the atom, once thought to be indivisable, can be broken down or split into component parts, too. Atoms consist of a nucleus or central part, and one or more electrons which revolve around the nucleus in a closed orbit or orbits, very similar to the orbits of the planets around our sun. The nucleus of an atom consists of various particles, such as mesons, protons, neutrons, etc. Each of these tiny particles is itself spinning around on its own individual axis, as well as orbiting in space, either inside the nucleus or outside of it. The axis of each particle has a very definite wobble or "nutation." *The nutation rate of all particles making up the universe is the same, on the physical plane of existence, which is the one where we presently exist. This nutation or vibration rate is fixed, and cannot be altered in any way.** This fact is important to remember, for it is the basis for what is to follow.

---

*This information from *The Ultimate Frontier*, by Eklal Kueshana (The Stelle Group, Stelle, Illinois 60919).

Our Physical Environment

When you pick up a metal object, say a nail or bolt made of iron or steel, it feels heavy, solid, and not easily changed in shape. This is not because it really is solid, because it isn't. It is mostly empty space! This seems hard to believe, but scientists tell us that it is a fact. Each atom of iron, consisting of a nucleus with a number of orbiting electrons, occupies a vast amount of space compared to the actual volume of its components. In other words, it is the size of the orbits of its electrons that determines the size of the atom of iron. If you can visualize a piece of iron as atoms in mostly empty space, being held together by a force which chemists call a chemical bond, think of the tremendous force needed to give this piece of iron the qualities it has — rigidity, strength and resistance to bending or breaking. Truly, we still have much to learn about our universe!

The size of an atom is about one million million billionths of a gram in weight, and about .00000001 centimeter in diameter. These figures are meaningless to us except to confirm that they are tiny beyond our comprehension. And the size of an atom is the diameter of the orbits of its electrons, so it is still mostly empty space. Yet these minute particles are the building blocks of our entire universe. Another even more confusing fact is that the particles are not just pieces of material or substance like we are used to seeing, handling and contacting in our daily lives. Einstein's famous formula from his theory of relativity that made possible the discovery of the atomic energy, and resulted in the development of the atom bomb, is : *e equals mc square*, or energy equals mass times the square of the velocity. This shows that mass can also be energy, depending on whether it is moving in a straight line or in a closed orbit (to oversimplify it). Thus mass and energy are interchangeable, depending on the conditions of their environment. This theory of relativity has been demonstrated to be true by repeated experiments by many scientists, so it is no longer just theory. In view of this, we can go ahead on the assumption that matter and energy are interchangeable.

To help you visualize the vast distances involved in the orbits of the atomic electrons compared to their size, consider first the solar system. We will suppose that the sun and the planets are cut down to a size which we can more easily visualize. If the sun is one mile in diameter, the earth will be 48 feet in diameter, and 108 miles away from the sun. The planet farthest from the sun is Pluto, and on our scale model it will be 4200 miles from the sun. Now if you shrink this model down to atomic size, you get some idea of the amount of empty space in an atom compared to the size of its various components. Actually, the electrons in the atom are even farther apart in comparison to their volume than the components of the solar system. So there is plenty of room between the parts of an atom or molecule, and this fact is important to understand for the discussion in the next chapter. If you are interested in visualizing the solar system in its actual size, just multiply the figures given above by a factor of one million. For instance, the earth is about 8,000 miles in diameter, and about 93,000,000 miles from the sun. The sun is so large compared to any of the planets that its volume equals about 585 times that of all the planets combined. This compares with the nucleus of the atom, which contains most of the mass of the atom.

The following is quoted from The Ultimate Frontier*:

"Another vital part of our environment is the ether, which pervades all space in the universe, even inside the atom. The ether has very special properties not shared by other matter on the physical plane. It has several functions, one of which is to act as a medium for the transmittal of the whole spectrum of radiation of energy, from radio waves through infra-red, visible light, ultraviolet, x-rays and so on. It also transmits the energy of our thoughts and our actions, and records them permanently, somewhat like the electromagnetic vibrations recorded on the tape of a

---

*This information obtained, with permission, from The Ultimate Frontier, by Eklal Kueshana (published by The Stelle Group, Stelle, Illinois 60919).

tape recorder. Every thought and action of every entity since man was created, has been recorded and can be retrieved under the proper conditions. This record is called the Book of Life, or the Akashic Record, which is a word taken from the Sanskrit language. Our brain also stores such information as thoughts, actions and emotions electromagnetically in its memory bank.

"The energy stored in the ether is in a different form than either the potential or kinetic energy which we studied in high school physics. It might be called quiescent energy, because it can be converted by our thoughts into either energy or matter. People of highly developed intelligence and consciousness are able to precipitate physical objects directly from the ether, and in fact, as we shall learn later, this is the manner in which our entire universe was created."

Chapter Two
Edgar Cayce and Reincarnation

The atomic theory which was described in the preceding chapter was presented as a basis for an explanation of the mechanics of reincarnation. But before going into this, I would like to tell you a little about Edgar Cayce and the great work he did, because I believe that anyone who knows his story will learn, as he did, to believe in reincarnation.* Cayce himself did not believe in it until the amount of evidence in favor of it became overwhelming.

When I first heard of him, I assumed he was in the same class as entertainers, hypnotists and clairvoyants who performed for profit. Nothing could be farther from the truth. Cayce was a poor farm boy in Kentucky in the 1800's, and was not particularly bright in school. His ambition as a boy was to become a preacher, and he read the Bible every day, trying to read it all the way through once a year. But he did not realize his ambition to become a preacher because of the poor financial circumstances of his family, and he moved into town after completing the ninth grade in school. Here he worked first in a book store, then later as an insurance salesman.

---

*There are many books in print about Edgar Cayce. I recommend *There is a River* by Thomas Sugrue (Dell Publishing Co., New York City).

He learned by accident that he had clairvoyant ability, and began giving "readings" for people who came to him with their ailments. He never took any money for these services; he earned a living as a photographer, although he was always in poor financial straits. He married and had two sons, and his reputation grew as he helped more and more people, who came to him from increasingly great distances. After his first few readings, all his spoken words were taken down in shorthand, and later transcribed by typewriter. As his fame continued to grow, he closed his photography shop and devoted himself full time to the readings, charging enough to support his family.

His method of operation was simple and direct, performed without any gimmicks and only in private sessions. He would lie on a couch, remove his shoes, loosen his tie and put himself to sleep. Then his associate, who was someone he trusted, would ask him to examine the person involved in the reading, who could be present at the time or a thousand miles away. All Cayce would need would be the exact name, address, city and state of the person. He would say something like "yes, we have the body," and then he would go into a complete medical diagnosis, using medical terms and anatomical descriptions, giving the names of obscure drugs or therapy at times, or operations that he knew absolutely nothing about in his waking state. He gave over 30,000 readings during his lifetime, and while the percentage of correct diagnosis and cure was not 100 percent, it was not far from it. Those who came to him in the early days of his career were mostly those who had been told by their doctors that there was no hope for them, but Cayce was able to go directly to the source of the trouble, and in many cases tell them how to effect a cure. The recommendations in his readings covered the whole field of medicine, old and new. There are many books available about Cayce, and they are highly interesting reading.

During his readings Cayce often made references to former lives of persons for whom he was reading, and Cayce could not understand this, because he did not believe in reincarnation. But evidence piled up, with names, dates and places that were verifiable, until he finally had to come around to accepting it. For many years all his readings were for healing the sick, but in later years he was persuaded to give "life readings" which were for the purpose of exploring the past lives of his clients, in order that they might be able to correct personality traits or emotional disturbances. The records of all of Cayce's readings are on file and available to the public in a foundation established by him and his sons at Virginia Beach, Virginia, where he lived. He died in 1945 at the age of 67, feeling the strain and energy drain on his nervous system from taking as many as eight readings a day. He devoted his life to helping the sick, and could not bear to turn anyone away, whether they had the ability to pay or not. He never advertised or promoted his abilities, and if one of his clients was dissatisfied with his efforts, he was quick to refund whatever they had paid.

When Cayce started giving life readings, he had misgivings as to whether he was working for God or the devil in probing into the past, and whether reincarnation was in accordance with the teachings of Christianity. Since he had been taught the straight-laced orthodox teachings of that day, and had no knowledge of what might be going on in the outside world, in other religions and beliefs, he did not know that both Hinduism and Buddhism had taught reincarnation for many centuries.

It may be necessary to differentiate between reincarnation and transmigration, which is a human soul returning to earth after death to inhabit an animal body. When asked to explain reincarnation, the Cayce readings gave a clear explanation that the human soul spends some time on earth in the physical plane, and some time on the next plane, alternately, in order to attain further advancement in character, proficiency and knowledge. Since true knowledge can be gained only through experience, it takes many lifetimes to attain Egoic advancement and balance. A proper balance between practicality and idealism is essential in order to advance into higher consciousness, as will be elaborated later.

Cayce's uncertainty about the accuracy and validity of the material in his life readings caused him to do extensive research in the local library, and he found the readings to be in complete agreement with historical facts. The readings also gave much information about the lost continent of Atlantis, which sank beneath the Atlantic Ocean some 10,000 years ago. Cayce read the books available on this subject, and again found agreement with his readings. After Cayce's death, an explorer and writer wrote a book called *Atlantis*, in which he described his discovery, off the coast of Bimini Island in the Caribbean, of evidence of a lost civilization only twenty feet below the surface of the clear water. He found great blocks of stone, hand-crafted into cubes, and apparently used to construct a sea-wall which the author theorized probably went all the way around the island to keep out the rising water. The nearest place where such stone could have been found is in the Andes Mountains of South America.

During his readings while under self-hypnosis, Cayce used words to describe the past lives of his clients that were completely foreign to his vocabulary, and not even of general knowledge to people of his time. But on consulting an encyclopedia, dictionary or history book, they could usually be found to apply to the period in which the events took place. Another fascinating feature of the readings was that they were able to foretell the character and personality traits of new-born infants or young children who had not yet developed Egoically. These findings have been verified in many cases and found to be accurate years later. In these cases the readings stated that the past-life attributes of the child would be carried over into the present life, for additional experience in correcting problems and improving overall character. The concept of Egoic advancement is evident in the readings, as is the concept of Christ's teachings of love for God and for all humanity, and of the Golden Rule. This is what finally convinced Cayce that the readings were actually true and valid. Since all other religions teach essentially the same simple precepts, this would seem to give us the real purpose of life — Egoic advancement and love. It would also bring all religions together, if they would bury all their petty differences and return to Christ's simple principles. It would also bring science and religion closer together, if science would explore the universal laws of nature and the human mind with the same effort they now devote to technology. We have become a materialistic world, at the expense of our spiritual advancement and knowledge.

The files of Edgar Cayce have a wealth of information that has not been researched. It would be an excellent place to start.

Chapter Three
The Mechanics of Reincarnation*

Now let's go back to the piece of iron we talked about in chapter one. We said it was composed of molecules which in turn were composed of atoms, and spaced widely apart rather than packed tightly together into a solid mass, as one might expect. It is the force of chemical attraction or chemical bond which holds the molecules in a certain relationship, rather than their close proximity to one another. Our bodies are similarly constructed of molecules and atoms, with similarly large distances between the various molecules and atoms of the substances of which our bodies are made.

There is plenty of room for another body to slip inside or coexist with our physical body in the same space, and this is actually the case. In fact, according to the philosophy of The Brotherhoods, there are four bodies existing within the same boundaries as our physical body. One of these is the Astral body, which is the one that goes along with our consciousness when we die and move to the Astral plane of existence. It is merely a shell, for identification purposes only, since we don't need to eat or sleep in the Astral plane.

---

*This entire chapter contins information taken, with permission, from *The Ultimate Frontier* by Eklal Kueshana.

There is also the Vital body, which is a pattern in the ether of our physical body, and which controls its shape and construction. It ensures that as the body cells die and are replaced, the body will maintain its original configuration. (Incidentally, the body cells are completely renewed about every seven years.) The fourth body is the Mental body, and it is not fully defined or developed until we have attained advancement to higher consciousness mentally and spiritually, and are ready to advance to the Mental plane of existence. These four bodies of ours, the physical, astral, vital and mental, all nestle comfortably together — one inside the other, so to speak — without interference or conflict, each having its specific purpose and function.

Nutation rate is the name given by scientists for the wobble of the axis of a particle of matter as it spins around. We mentioned this earlier, and now we are ready to apply it to our understanding of how reincarnation works. According to The Brotherhoods, there are seven planes of existence — our physical plane being one of them — and while all the planes of existence are composed of the same atoms or building blocks, each of the planes requires these atoms to have a different nutation rate. The atoms in the physical plane have the lowest nutation rate, and those of the Vital plane have the next higher rate, which is one octave higher. Each of the other planes has a nutation rate progressively an octave higher than the one below it. The first four planes of existence, in order of nutation rate, are called the Human Life Wave, for reasons which will be explained later. The other three planes of existence are the Angelic, Archangelic and Celestial planes.

The steps in nutation rate are similar to the pitch in music, where each octave is twice the vibration rate or frequency of the octave below it. Residents occupying the Astral plane are able to perceive what goes on in the planes below them, but those in the physical plane cannot perceive events or conditions in the planes above them. Similarly, all the planes of existence are able to perceive events in all the planes below them in nutation rate. Egos called Adepts need not reincarnate when they have learned all there is to know of the Physical plane, and have advanced their consciousnesses to a high level. When they have reached the state of advancement where they function on the Mental plane, human Egos are called Masters and are ready to advance to the next plane, which is the Angelic plane. But the Brotherhoods teach that they do not advance immediately: they will all advance at the same time, and in the meantime will utilize their abilities to assist other Egos who are still struggling on the path to perfection to advance into the Mental plane.

According to the Brotherhoods' philosophy, all Egos were created at the same time, about one million years ago. Of these, about one-sixth have been on Earth in the Physical plane at any one time, the rest residing in the Astral plane and waiting for the right opportunity to reincarnate into the Physical plane in order to continue their Egoic advancement. Incarnation occurs at birth, or slightly before or after birth. An Ego selects his parents and the time and place of birth in order to have an environment conducive to his further development. Once he is in a physical body, the conscious mind takes over, starting life experiences anew, and he no longer knows anything about his past lives. An Ego can and does incarnate hundreds and even thousands of times, each time adding a little to his character and to the knowledge stored in his subconscious. Sometimes, by his actions, thoughts and emotions, he backtracks in his growth.

There have been four great civilizations during the course of our planet's existence, and two of them were more highly developed both technologically and spiritually than our present one. The first was on a large continent in the Pacific Ocean, called Lemuria, or Mu. It flourished for fifty thousand years, and finally decayed because its people failed to live up to the natural laws of the universe. This continent submerged into the Pacific, and later a new civilization began in the Atlantic, also on an island that is now below the surface of the ocean. This was called Atlantis, and this civilization lasted about ten thousand years. (If you would like to read more about the dawn of civilization, read *The Sun Rises* by Dr. Robert D. Stelle, which tells about life on Lemuria.)

The Astral plane, where Egos reside after their physical bodies die, has been described by clairvoyants who are able to get glimpses of it at times, and by persons who have "died" temporarily and been revived while on the operating table, or after a near-fatal accident or illness. It is remarkable how these descriptions all coincide in important details, telling of a place of great beauty and light, incomparable with anything on the physical plane. They also agree that one has an intense feeling of peace, contentment and happiness. The Astral plane, like the Physical plane, has many levels, and is inhabited by Egos of different levels of advancement, from the lowest to the highest. An Ego will go to the level which corresponds with his level of advancement, spiritually as well as mentally.

Time is a function of the Physical plane, and in the Astral plane there is no time as we know it. Events do not follow one another in chronological sequence as they do here on Earth. This is the reason that Egos who are able to project their consciousnesses into the Astral plane, such as clairvoyants, are able to see into the past and future. Also, Egos of like mental and spiritual qualities tend to be drawn together, so you will most likely find some of your old friends and relatives there when you arrive on the Astral plane.

Now that we know something about the death of the physical body, we lose much of our fear, for death becomes an adventure to be anticipated with pleasure. We can think of the upper Astral plane as heaven, and the lower levels as hell. It is up to us which level we select, through our thoughts and actions while we are still incarnate. Quoting from the Bible, "To enter heaven, you must bring it with you."

Reincarnation has had and now has many supporters among the best minds in the world. In olden times, some were afraid to come out strongly for it because of fear of ridicule or reprisal. In a later chapter we will find out about the organization called the Brotherhoods, which has been active for 20,000 years, and is composed of the wisest and most learned men and women of all the eras through which civilization has passed. Reincarnation is one of the cornerstones of their philosophy. It is the only philosophy that can explain satisfactorily all the mysteries of the universe, that can bring religion and science together, and that embraces all religions and all people.

Besides the logical arguments in favor of reincarnation, there is something else — an intuitive feeling that it is right, that it is the truth. I have this feeling, and I think many others must also have it, or it would not have gained acceptance among so many people.

Chapter Four
Karma

The word *karma* is becoming increasingly familiar to people today, because of the popularity of occult books and widespread interest in the occult. It is a Sanskrit word, and means something very much like "action and reaction." It can also be translated literally as "carry-over," and it has this meaning when applied to the Akashic Record, carried over from one incarnation to another. There is a universal law which governs all our thoughts, emotions, actions and events over which we have no control. We already know there is such a law governing events in the spheres of science — mathematics, chemistry, physics and other fields — but this is also true of the entire universe, in all ways, physically, mentally and spiritually. *Karma* is the manifestation of this law, and it can work in either a positive or negative direction.

While it may seem that karma is sometimes working against us, it is really always working for us. If we need a lesson of some kind, to teach us to develop a quality in which we are deficient, we must work out the karmic situation in order to give us the life experience we need for advancement and knowledge. The Cayce books have many instances of the operation of karma; one of the best of these books is *Many Mansions* by Gina Cerminara, published by Signet Books. Portions of this chapter have been taken, with permission, from her book.

Karmic reaction does not always appear during the same lifetime in which the karmic action took place. It may not surface for several lifetimes, until the most favorable conditions arise. So there is no way we can tell in advance what is going to befall us, until we go to the Astral plane. Then we can examine our karmic record, and make plans to improve it on our next sojourn on the physical plane. Of course there are merits as well as demerits, and for each good deed or kind thought that helps to improve the general welfare of all concerned, we balance out unkind thoughts and actions. Also, thoughts can be returned to us as actions. For instance, derisive laughter at someone's misfortune might bring the same misfortune to the one who laughed. A helping hand to an unfortunate one would chalk up a karmic plus in the record. A study was recently made in several large cities to find out what the reaction of the average citizen would be to a child's appeal to them for help. It is hard to believe, but about three-fourths of them turned down or brushed aside the child's appeals. It shows that there is a great deal of room for improvement in our relationships with our fellow men. Think of the karmic debits built up by these individuals!

Not only individuals, but also groups and even governments build up karmic records. Some nations have such a large karmic indebtedness that they will never be able to redeem themselves. Thus they are doomed to eventual destruction. In this regard, I would like to put in a word for a little country in Central America which I visited a few years ago, Costa Rica. In my estimation, this country is outstanding in many respects. Its people are descended from the Spanish Conquistadores, who massacred most of the Indians living there when the land was invaded. Yet, today the people as a whole are intelligent, industrious, kind and gentle. The literacy rate is the highest in Latin America, and the income level is also one of the highest, and growing annually. Their government is democratic, stable and honest. They have no military forces, spending their income instead on public services. The climate is almost ideal for any taste. On the Central Plateau, where one-half the population lives, the temperature varies slightly around 78 degrees, winter and summer. They have a wet and dry season much like California, except at different times of the year. On the seacoasts it is more tropical, with lush vegetation, and in the high mountains, which go up to over 11,000 feet, it can be chilly. From the way in which the Costa Ricans manage their country and their lives, I think they have the best karmic record of any country I know of.

Karma should not be thought of as a punishment or reward. It is simply a law of the universe that governs our thoughts and actions, the same way the law of gravity keeps us from flying off into space, and the other natural laws keep all things in balance, spiritually as well as physically. It is all part of God's Great Plan for the universe.

We who are here on Earth going about our daily lives are oblivious to any other plane of existence, because it is outside our consciousness. But as we learn that many things exist of which we are not conscious because of our very limited senses, we can begin to realize that other planes may exist of which we are unaware. It is possible that life on the Astral plane is the real life, not life on the Physical plane, and that our life here is only to test us, to give us experience to improve our character and balance. I think both are real lives — they are just different, but one is just as real as the other. We must bear in mind constantly that in order to escape reincarnating back to Earth periodically, we must, among other things, eliminate all our negative karma, or karmic debits. To do this, we must control our thoughts and actions, as all actions start with thoughts.

Karma can occur in many different ways, sometimes directly and sometimes symbolically. A man who kills another may himself be killed; one who causes much bloodshed may in later life find himself anemic. A young man plagued with bed-wetting since infancy found from the Cayce readings that in a former life he had officiated at a form of torture called "stool-dipping," in which witches were dipped into cold water. After learning the cause of his problem, he was cured by working on his subconscious to reprogram it.

Christ said, "Whatsoever ye sow, so shall ye reap." We can reap the rewards of fulfilment, happiness and inner peace by surrounding ourselves with an environment favorable to these things. We are now living in an environment that we created ourselves, in this lifetime and in previous ones, and we are now creating the environment in which we will live in the future. Our thoughts, emotions and actions regulate our progress toward this goal. The afflictions we are now bearing we brought on ourselves; no one else is responsible for them. Our finer qualities are also the result of our own efforts, and ours alone. This is simply the universal law of action and reaction, cause and effect, or karma, and cannot be by-passed or avoided. But if we follow the karmic law, it can be of enormous benefit to us, and can give us the ability to draw other desirable factors into our environment through the power of our thoughts.

When we realize the validity of reincarnation and karma, we begin to see that the Bible makes more sense. Christianity teaches us that Christ died for our salvation, and forgave us all our sins. But it does not teach us that we must redeem ourselves, and that no one will do it for us. Forgiving does not mean cancelling our sins, and if we are to advance on the path to perfection, we must constantly work at it. Having learned this much, we can go forward with confidence and faith in the future. There is no reason to fear future karma, because karma is always just, and no karma will ever be more than the Ego can bear. And it is always for the good of the Ego, to enable him to learn the lesson he needs to attain a better life. According to the

Cayce readings, a spiritual deficiency plays an important part in the karmic debits of most people. We must realize that we are immature spiritually, and we should approach the working out of a karmic problem in a spirit of humble willingness rather than rebellion. We do not need to accept every karmic situation with resignation, either, but should try to alleviate it by eliminating the underlying cause. For instance, allergies caused by karmic conditions in the past can sometimes be cured by mental suggestion. A positive spiritual attitude is also needed, assuring the subconscious that there is no longer any valid reason for continuing the reaction, since all karmic conditions have been fulfilled. The correct mental attitude is very important in order for the body's healing and recuperative powers to be effective.

The Cayce files show that such spiritual qualities as selfishness, separativeness, lack of brotherly love, or lack of patience and kindliness are considered sins that require karmic correction. Man's preoccupation with his physical body rather than the spirit has given his Ego an incorrect conception of physical and spiritual balance. All through the Cayce readings, the concept of brotherly love is evident as the most essential factor in man's spiritual awareness.

The marriage relationship between man and woman is the most sacred and the most fulfilling that we can experience on the Physical plane of existence. It is also the most apt to have karmic consequences, for it is the best opportunity we have to show our true natures, our talents and our faults, and our characters. It is our best opportunity to weed out the bad qualities of character and fill in the deficiencies. In short, it is our best chance to attain consciousness growth. The conception and rearing of children is a God-given opportunity to demonstrate the unselfishness, love and affection inherent in all of us. The creation of a home is the single most important thing we can do to further the Egoic growth of ourselves and of the world around us.

The Cayce readings do not specify whether women should make a home or seek a career, but seem to advise in each case on its individual merits. But there is no doubt from the readings that a home and children is considered the most important. One thing mentioned several times is the necessity for a pregnant woman to not only prepare her body for the proper development of the child, but even more importantly to train her mind to accept the right kind of thoughts and to prepare herself spiritually for the birth of the child. One reason this spiritual preparation is so important is that the soul coming into the body will pick out the parents with great care, in order to create an environment conducive to its further Egoic development. Since Egos generally pick environments and parents that are familiar to them, and that contain the conditions necessary for them to attain better balance, the same Egos may, and usually do, get back into the same families as in previous incarnations, although not in the same relationships. When a medium once told an acquaintance of mine that her brother had been her husband in a former incarnation, it sounded like a product of the medium's imagination to me. But now I can see that it could very well be possible.

Many of our characteristics which are usually described as hereditary are actually karmic in origin, and have been carried over from past life experiences. This includes such things as vocational bents, musical talent and artistic ability. It can also apply to physical attributes and problems such as deformities, illness and birth defects, which may or may not be karmic. So it is not correct to assume that all the conditions we face are karmically caused. Although the universal law of karma regulates all events of importance, it does not exercise control over every action in minutest detail, since man is free to go his own way and make his own decisions. But karma acts as a corrective force when we stray from the path of consciousness growth. And it is always acting for us, never against us. Should we try to help others with their problems if we suspect that they may be working out a karmic situation? Apparently, some Hindus say that if they help such a person, they incur negative karma, and so does the recipient of the help. But this is not the way of Christ's teachings; which ask us to lend a helping hand, to love our neighbors, and to live unselfishly for service to others. There are times when we can see clearly that it would be best for all concerned not to interfere — and this is when we must use discrimination and good judgement. But I cannot see any excuse for turning down an opportunity to be of service to someone with the excuse that it might cause us to lose karmic credits.

One might say that if reincarnation is true, why does not the Bible mention it? It does, in several places, but in a round-about way. Another reason might well be that the Bible has gone through so many hands before being brought together into one volume, and through so many translations, that it was almost bound to suffer somewhat in the process. In one case a ruler who had the writings in his possession had about ninety percent of them burned, because they did not fit his idea of the truth. It is also possible that Christ and His disciples did not want to throw too much at the people of that day, for fear of giving them more than they could handle. In fact, it is more than a lot of people can handle today! But what we have discussed so far has only scratched the surface of the mysteries of the universe.

Chapter Five
The Brotherhoods

The story of the Brotherhoods is an amazing one. It is told in detail in the book *The Ultimate Frontier* by Eklal Kueshana (available in paperback at most bookstores).* As we have mentioned previously, the Brotherhoods were organized about 20,000 years ago, during the civilization of Atlantis, and have been active ever since. One of their purposes was to assist mankind in his struggles on the path to perfection. The Atlantians had become divided, during their development, into two classes, one idealistic and the other overly materialistic. The first of the twelve Brotherhoods was organized to try to bring these two opposite factions into balance, and They set up schools to teach the Atlantians. Another task of the Brotherhoods was to gather together all the knowledge and information accumulated by man, and preserve it for future generations. At the present time, the Brotherhoods have schools in every part of the world. Men and women of all races are involved, and the Brotherhoods' activities have made it possible for man to evolve to his present state of advancement.

The Brotherhoods have always operated quietly, behind the scenes. In fact, until recently it has been necessary for them to meet in secrecy for fear of retaliation or abuse from those in power. In 1963 they decided that the time had

---

*Information contained in this chapter was taken from the book, *The Ultimate Frontier*, by Eklal Kueshana (The Stelle Group, Stelle Illinois, Cabery P.O. 60919), with their permission.

come for them to reveal their mysteries to the general public, and accordingly the book mentioned above was published. The twelve Brotherhoods are divided into two groups: the five Greater Brotherhoods, who operate in the Mental plane of existence, and the seven Lesser Brotherhoods, whose concern is with the Egos in the Physical plane. Their membership includes the greatest men of every era — Christ, Moses, Buddha, Mohammed, Confucius and other great religious leaders of ancient times — as well as the Prophets, who were all students of the Brotherhoods, except for one. Many of the founders of our republic, including Washington, Madison, Franklin and Jefferson, were members or students of the Brotherhoods. Our country was deliberately planned by the Brotherhoods to be the first republic in which a free and democratic government could flourish, in order to form a guiding light for the oppressed peoples of the world. Our present sad state of affairs in this country is not the result of any fault in the system, but is because too many people have lost the spirit of our forefathers, the spirit of honesty, cooperation and unselfishness toward one's fellow man, for the benefit of all the people.

One of the greatest feats performed by the Brotherhoods in ancient times was the construction of the Great Pyramid of Gizeh. It was scientifically designed and oriented, and built to withstand the elements for many centuries in order to provide a lasting record of man's knowledge in the universal language of mathematics. To the few who have been able to read it, it gives fundamental mathematical principles, astronomical distances, a measurement standard for distances on our planet, and it foretells important events on Earth. All dimensions of the pyramid are exact to within a small fraction of an inch. The men who built the pyramid were members of a white race in Ethiopia. They came to Egypt and infiltrated the government until they finally were able to elect a ruler, who then began construction of the Great Pyramid. After it was completed, they split into two groups and slowly faded out of the picture. One of the groups went to what is now England, where they set up the great monoliths at Stonehenge.

The Great Pyramid was not built as a tomb, as were the other smaller pyramids. One purpose of building it was to have a secure place to store the irreplaceable records of the Brotherhoods. They met in an underground room between the paws of the Sphinx, and it was here that the Great Plan of the Brotherhoods was formulated. The Great Plan is arranged to coincide with the events taking place in the next twenty years or so, which They prophesy as including the climax of World War III or Armageddon in the year 1998, followed in the year 2000 by a great cataclysm inundating the Earth, including volcanoes, earthquakes and upheavals all over the Earth. A shifting of the Earth's plates or crust will occur from gravitational forces caused by a shift in the Earth's axis. This in turn will cause a shifting of the Earth's ice caps, and the whole thing will be triggered by the fact that all the planets will be aligned in such a position as to cause the maximum gravitational effect on our planet. The exact date is supposed to be May 5, 2000 A.D., and the Brotherhoods are putting plans into effect to prepare for the event by salvaging what is possible or desirable in order to start a new civilization on a new continent as yet still beneath the sea. They expect to eliminate the errors of the past, so that the new Nation of God will survive and prosper for a thousand years in an environment which will be conducive to the advancement of mankind to perfection and oneness with God. Christ himself will lead this Nation, and there will be no evil, and nothing to interfere with the peace and tranquility needed for Egoic growth. This will be the millenium spoken of in the Bible. The Stelle Group, mentioned earlier, has built a community at Stelle, Illinois, about sixty miles south of Chicago, and is presently training its members, under the guidance of the Brotherhoods, to learn the technology and other things that will be necessary to know when the time comes to form the new civilization. The community is complete with schools, homes, industry and farms in order to become a self-sufficient entity as soon as possible. They publish a semi-monthly newsletter which they will mail on request, telling of their activities and progress.

There are twelve degrees of Brotherhood, from the first, or Initiate, to the twelfth, or Master. A Brother between eighth and eleventh degrees is called an Adept, and when one has reached this level of consciousness and knowledge, he is no longer required to reincarnate into the Physical plane, as he has learned all there is to know on that plane of existence.

One of the Brotherhoods' objectives is to combat the efforts of the "Black Mentalists." These are discarnate Egos who were the priests of former eras, who were able to attain clairvoyant powers and now seek to enslave the minds of any and all Egos who are susceptible to them. More will be discussed on this subject in a later chapter. The Black Mentalists are apparently having a ball with all the millions of young people who are now taking drugs, which make them easy targets. This is also one good reason why one should never allow himself to be hypnotized, as in this state he has allowed another to take control of his mind. Other discarnate Egos from the lower Astral plane can also take advantage of a situation like this and command the person's physical body. This may be the explanation of being "possessed." If one ever feels that such a thing may be happening to him, he should pray for protection. God's power is always greater than that of the Black Mentalists, because they are only human Egos out of the Physical plane.

The Brotherhoods' philosophy of reincarnation differs from that of the churches, who teach resurrection of the physical body. The Brotherhoods say there is no need for the physical body after we leave the Physical plane, in that we have our Astral bodies, which never age or deteriorate.

The Brotherhoods are also battling the Black Mentalists on another front, the relationship between man and woman. Love is not the problem, for there will never be too much love in the world. God Himself is pure love, and Christ is that divine love made manifest to men. The love that a man feels for his God, his wife, his child and his neighbor are all the same. However, toward his mate man demonstrates yet another facet of his nature, sex. The churches will tell you that love is pure, because it arises from the mind, but that sex is vile because it arises from the body. Sex is our most powerful emotion, and because it can cause so much mischief it has been labeled by society as filthy, with the hope that man will disown and obliterate it. Sex in itself is not filthy. The animals all have the mating urge, and when man was created by the Angels, They lovingly created human bodies to experience deep emotional fulfilment during the sex act, and designed the sex act to be a unifying expression of tenderness between mates. A marriage without sexual expression is hollow. Unfortunately, sex has been made into a very effective tool of the Black Mentalists for disillusioning souls, by debasing sex as being the most romantic when it is forbidden.

Sex is a two-edged sword. It can lead one to depths of despair, depravity and psychological fears which can preclude happiness for a lifetime. Or, in its Angelic dignity, it can elevate one to heights of love and marital bliss. How one uses sex may well determine his whole outlook on life. A man's sexual morality is a reliable barometer of his overall morality. The effective power of his intellect to control his sex drive so it will be wholly beneficial is an indication of his command of and control of his other drives and appetites.

Intellect must command man's emotional nature if his desires are to serve him in an ordered, self-disciplined way. His self-esteem and spiritual strength arise from control over nature, and over his own human nature. Self-discipline is the seed of Egoic growth. Morality and karma are closely related, and immoral actions are those which are not for the benefit of all concerned, which is the same definition as for sin.

Chapter Six
The Bible

In spite of the shortcomings of the churches' interpretations of Christianity, which are not always the real truth, the churches have brought the teachings of Christ to the people, and this has been of great benefit to them spiritually. The concepts of hell-fire and damnation, saving our souls merely by asking Christ to forgive our sins without working out our karma, and of returning to our physical bodies for everlasting life after death, have all been mentioned previously. These are all teachings of the Black Mentalists, who have thus shackled the peoples' minds with these ideas, and stifled their God-given right to think for themselves. The churches, by their use of dogma and rituals, have limited man's God-given powers of reason and intellect, and have limited the priests' power to teach the people by the rules of the particular denomination, so they are not allowed to teach anything beyond that point.

The Bible, too, is subject to various interpretations, and it should be read with intelligence and the realization that some of it was written in allegorical style, and cannot be taken literally, word for word. But the men who wrote it were inspired by enlightenment from God, and what they wrote was the truth. The recent discovery of the Dead Sea scrolls has added more evidence to the validity of the historical facts in the Old Testament.

Man has been given the intellect and common sense to interpret and understand the Bible. For instance, morality is not a matter of simple compliance with rules. Happiness results from intellectual moral integrity, not from rules set up by an external agent. Any logically-minded person will arrive at the same conclusion as the wise men who wrote the Bible. Every rule, commandment and admonition in the Bible outlines the path for the most serene and satisfying way of life. The method by which one can gain and maintain communion with the Lord is written for the wise to discern, and the full panoply of karmic pitfalls are warned against and entertainingly dramatized. These are intended to minimize one's karmic indebtedness, with its attendant sorrow and misfortune. An absence of negative karma is essential to our Egoic advancement, and this is the reason that the Higher Beings have made such an issue of sin in the Bible. To lead the good life is divinely selfish, for one gains for himself in every way. But in helping others on their path to advancement, it should not be done at the expense of one's own Egoic growth, for an Ego can only advance by himself — no one else can do it for him. Our help should be in the form of trying to provide a better environment for another's progress.

If one has reservations about some of the stories in the Bible, here are some explanations:

In the fifth chapter of Matthew, second verse, it is explained that the story of Adam and Eve is an allegory describing the first race of man. Cain, symbolizing the farmer, overcame Abel, the nomad, showing that man had ceased his nomadic way of life, and had settled down to till the soil. This stability on the land gave rise to civilization.

Noah's Ark dramatizes the submersion of Lemuria, or Mu. This was a vast continent located where the Pacific Ocean now lies.

The Tower of Babel symbolized the far-flung world.

Abram is likely wholly symbolic, as his name means Father, God of Mu. Even St. Paul referred to some of this episode as an allegory. The fact that Melchizedek (Christ) was brought into the story of Abram, and was referred to as the King of Salem, only increases the likelihood that Genesis is allegorical, for in Timothy's epistle to Hebrews 7:2, it is explained that Melchizedek is the King of Peace. Salem means peace in the language of Mu. It is therefore possible that Abram signifies Jehovah, for Timothy brings out the point that even the Chief of Angels is less than Melchizedek.

Incidentally, Jerusalem was originally Herosalem, which means God of Peace. All of Genesis is an esoteric allegorical parody in which only one real historic character of note is recorded: Joseph, counsel to Pharaoh, whose tale is deeply symbolic of Christ's advent and forgiveness of man.

The great confusion in the early books of the Bible arose in the hands of Ezra, the priest who translated the writings of Moses from Egyptian into Hebrew about 600 years after Moses withdrew from his people. Moses wrote his book in high caste Egyptian. Ezra and other learned priests of the Jews sought to translate the sacred papyri, but they were unaware that the Egyptian hieroglyphics carried two meanings; a priestly secret meaning, and a common meaning. The Jewish scholars were doomed at the start. Had they been Brothers, we would now have a true story of creation in our Bible. But Ezra's scholars were power-seeking priests subject to the Black Mentalists. They altered what they could not understand, and made up what they could not fill in. Their fabrications were designed to perpetuate the priesthood in power, which was similar to what happened centuries later when those in power sought to call the divine right of kings part of the scriptures.

The net result of Ezra's perfidy was to withhold from the world the last great gift of true knowledge and history handed down to us from the Brotherhoods through Moses. The same archives of the Brotherhoods had been drawn upon by the Pharaoh Aknaton to bring about a renaissance in Egypt just prior to Moses' birth. This was part of the information later given by Christ to the Apostles. Christ and the Apostles had to be guarded in their teachings and writings. Christ could not go counter to the Bible, or the Jews would have rejected Him. What follows is a synopsis of events leading up to the second advent of Christ, the great cataclysm, and the formation of the new Kingdom or Nation of God, as foretold by the Hebrew Prophets of the Old and New Testament.

We of the present generation are very fortunate in that we are living at a time when world events are shaping up rather quickly according to the prophesies in the Bible, and we are able to observe these events as if on a stage, with ourselves as the audience. At a certain point, however, we will become participants in the drama, if we are still here in the flesh at that time.

All this sounds fantastic, and it is. But it is all in the Bible, and the Prophets who made these predictions, some as long as 3,000 years ago, were speaking the word of God, not their own fantasies. Their uncanny accuracy in predicting future events that have already taken place is the proof that God is speaking through them. Hundreds of prophesied events have come to pass, even though the Prophets were scoffed at and ridiculed, sometimes thrown into jail or murdered. All of the four civilizations of the ancient world — Babylon, Persia, Greece and Rome — had their prophets, but the ones who wrote the Bible were the ones who always had the right answers. For this reason, their predictions for events which have yet to happen should be considered very carefully and seriously.

Many scholars have studied the prophesies in the Bible, and have come up with different interpretations. This is because some have overlooked key factors in the puzzle, while others have made allegorical conclusions from passages that are in plain language. An excellent book on the

The Bible   51

subject is *The Late Great Planet Earth*, by Hal Lindsey and C. S. Carlson. It makes logical deductions, and explains the Biblical text in plain modern language.*
Some of the events that have been prophesied for our generation, and are already falling into place, are: the scattering of the Jews to the four corners of the earth, and their subsequent return to their homeland and formation of their new nation, the State of Israel; the emergence of Russia as a world power, from the mere collection of barbarous tribes existing at the time of the prophecy; the domination of third-world countries in Africa to form a communist bloc (now in progress); the gradual moral decay throughout the world; the drift away from Christ in the churches, through "modern" interpretations of His teachings; and the present boom in the occult, witchcraft and other metaphysical trends, including devil-worship and black magic. Prophesies which are still to come are continued and increasing tension in the Middle East, with Egypt finally starting the ball rolling by invading Israel; Russia will then take advantage of the opportunity to step in and attack Israel from the north. But Russia, true to her tradition, will also double-cross Egypt and the Black African countries, and take them all over, including all the Arab states. At the right moment, Christ will intervene to save Israel from complete annihilation, and Russia and her war machine will be destroyed.

This divine intervention will cause a spiritual awakening in the Israelites, and about one-third of them will be converted to Christ. In the meantime, however, a great ruler will appear from among the descendants of the Romans. He will be very popular with all people, and he will

---

*The following three paragraphs contain information taken, with permission, from *The Late Great Planet Earth*, by Hal Lindsey and C. C. Carlson. (Copyright © 1970, 1977 by Zondervan Publishing House, 1414 Lake Drive, S.E., Grand Rapids, Mich. 49506).

rule the Western World for three and a half years. He will be very successful in bringing peace and prosperity to all the countries, especially Israel, which will become very wealthy and powerful. But the Roman ruler is a tool of the devil (Black Mentalists), and when Israel and the Roman leader sign a pact giving Israel protection, it signifies the beginning of the seven-year period of Tribulations. After Russia's defeat, the ruler, who in the Bible is called Antichrist, assembles all the armies of the West to do battle with the approaching armies of the Communist Chinese, who number a staggering 200 million. The great battle is fought on the plains of the Holy Land, part of which is called Armageddon. This is the beginning of the end, and before the battle is over, Christ appears on Earth to stop the slaughter before every person on Earth is killed.

The believers on Earth will be protected by Christ, and will be removed miraculously prior to the period of the Tribulations. They will not have to endure the terror of these times. The Antichrist will become a cruel despot, forcing people to worship him as God. Those who refuse will be dealt with as other dictators deal with dissidents, including wholesale murder. Natural disasters will multiply in frequency, including earthquakes, tidal waves, torrential rains, volcanic eruptions, draughts and pestilence.

When Armageddon begins, even those who think they are safe will find no safety. When the great cataclysm comes, whole continents will dip beneath the seas, cities will be destroyed, and the geography of the world will be altered. The Bible says fire and brimstone will destroy people everywhere, with great pollution. This could be their way of describing nuclear warfare, but the Bible also says that every volcano on Earth will erupt.

Apparently the United States will not play a major role in this fight, but will be just one of the countries under the leadership of the Antichrist, which will include ten countries of western Europe. This confederacy will be organized during the first half of the seven-year period of the Tribulations, probably starting with the European Common Market, its nine members soon to be joined by Greece.

The new Kingdom of God will already have been started on an island in the Pacific Ocean, and after the great cataclysm will be moved to the new continent which will rise where Mu once was, and the new Kingdom of God will be founded there.*

---

*Information contained in the above chapter was taken, with permission, from *The Ultimate Frontier* by Eklal Kueshana (The Stelle Group, Stelle Illinois, Cabery P.O. 60919).

Chapter Seven
Immorality In The Business World

It has been mentioned that the democratic system in America is breaking down because of the attitudes of many of the people composing it. Following is a condensed version of material taken from *The Ultimate Frontier* and another book, *None Dare Call It Conspiracy*, by Gary Allen, published by Concord Press. There are some startling disclosures here that every thinking person should be aware of.

First, quoting from *The Ultimate Frontier*: "Some influence groups have managed to have prices manipulated to their own advantage, to the detriment of their competitors and suppliers. These are the very things pursued for the love of shrewd business, and all too many men pride themselves on pulling a shady deal. They can influence legislation and government policy ruinous to their competitors, and that is the kind of manipulation clever operators gloat over. Fraudulent business practices that are barely within the law have become so widespread that they are inexorably undermining the commercial structure. Misleading advertising, salesmen who misrepresent contracts, the manufacture of sleazy merchandise, and planned obsolescence are but a few of the extremely wasteful and exhorbitant methods which have gained popularity among buisnesses. Each is out to exploit a captive market of ignorant suckers.

"In the United States we have come to the point of selling hokum to one another. Big business today is conducted more and more in an alcoholic haze. Purchase contracts or sales agreements are signed in nightclubs or on the bar of a cocktail lounge. The purchasing agent selects the seller who offers the best entertainment, or the biggest rebates for his pocket. The interests of the buyer's firm are not served, and the ultimate consumer pays the tab. Good value and efficient service have been relegated to the background, while expense-account partying have taken their place. Business conducted by questionable influence is bragged about, by men who really should be ashamed. But theirs is a need to triumph in a jungle of double-dealing transactions. Such men view the ideals of democracy as giving them the freedom to grab whatever they can. To them, freedom of opportunity means every man has the right to gouge his way to the top, regardless of the station of his birth.

"Business is the principle contact a man has with his fellows. He spends more time at work than he does at home with his family and friends. Nowhere else is all man's activities and duties tested so frequently as in business. The continual opportunity to demonstrate one's moral integrity should be met with scrupulous adherence to the laws of karma. All money transactions involve the exchange of karmic credits, and should be handled with respect and care. All business must eventually realize that all business conduction is divine activity. Government also falls into the same category, and deserves the same attention to moral values and efficiency. Nations today have behaved as badly toward one another as have businessmen toward one another. But then, one of the main purposes of government today is to provide protection for business interests. Cartels and monopolies on the international level supercede all considerations of war and patriotism. During World War II, munitions were being sold between enemies, graft-hungry officials winking at questionable shipments to neutral countries for transfer into enemy hands. Millions of German and American boys followed their respective flags, even unto death. But at the highest business level, there are no national considerations — profits come first. It is the lust for money and power that destroys men.

"Communist Russia is a socialist dictatorship, the head of which in the name of the people, does in fact personally possess for his own use, the entire nation and its workers. The aristocracy of himself and his lieutenants share the fantastic loot, and the privilege which attends it. Hitler was the product of a grand experiment, which back-fired. Powerful industrialists of Britain and the United States conspired to control that dictator. A more fascinating aspect of that plan was to have the workers joined into an all-inclusive labor union, which would be controlled by the same dictator. Hitler, being the leader of the National Socialist Labor Party, would have dual control of government policy, and the workers. The big industrialists reasoned that were they to direct Hitler to dictate laws conducive to tremendous profits for them, they would have solved management's biggest problem, and especially the demands for human rights from the laborers. The police-state tactics of Hitler made strikes and riots a crime against the State, and an affront to their glorious leader. Germany was to be an experiment, which, if successful, would be extended throughout the world. All of Germany was to be reduced to the status of an industrial slave camp. Among the several political parties fomenting in Germany, Hitler's looked like the best for their plans, but they did not reckon with Hitler's personality. He too could see how well their plan would work, so he decided to go it alone, for his own glory and Germany's profit. Hitler signed Germany's death warrant when he prohibited the withdrawal of funds from Germany, except in very small amounts annually. This act was tantamount to confiscation of foreign capital, and the big industrialists moved to retaliate. Hitler nearly made his idea work, and the world will be plagued by his imitators for a long time to come. His method of coming into power, his reign of terror, his confiscation of private property, his denial of human rights and justice, and his ruthless consolidation of power, and the control of daily living, will be the world's legacy from Hitler and his backers, and it could happen here.

"The Brotherhoods are acutely aware of all such matters. They have collected written records of every civilization since the dawn of civilization on Lemuria. Their specific assignment from Melchizedek is to analyze and correlate every factor pertinent to the causes and failures of man's every attempt to organize socially. The scenes and rationales of these many varied social orders were fantastically varied. Some worthwhile ideas have been found, but most are childishly impractical. The purpose of the correlation is to provide a sound basis for the Kingdom of God. This final great civilization must be flawless. No factors which can lead to later dissension or karmic imbalance will be allowed into the forming nation. The Brothers have done their work well, and when the time comes to proceed all will go smoothly, because all contingencies have been prepared for."

Gary Allen, in his well-documented book, tells how big business operates. Here is a brief summary:

There is an organization of influential men which has flourished and expanded for a hundred years, and yet which the average person has never heard of. It is called the Council on Foreign Relations, an innocent enough name. It includes most of the rich and powerful men of this country, including those in government, industry, the news media and international bankers and almost every important field of endeavor. It has included presidents, senators, representatives, judges and cabinet members and powerful bureaucrats. They meet in private, without any press coverage except what they themselves choose to release. By their ability to control the highest levels of government, industry and banking, they are able to wield tremendous power and influence. They can set interest rates, make the stock market go up or down, affect trade with other countries, regulate policies for handling our domestic affairs, and in general practically run the country — for their own benefit.

The Council on Foreign Relations is part of a world organization called the Round Table, which is based in Holland. It includes organizations similar to the CFR from most of the countries of western Europe. The Round Table is run by a few super-rich and powerful tycoons, and they are the ones who are really in a position to crack the whip. The international bankers, mostly in the United States plus the Rothschilds in England, have great power over the governments of the world, through their control of money. Since most governments are heavily in debt to them, including the United States, the banks can almost make or break a country, thereby setting their national policies.

The CFR and the Round Table can even start or stop a war, and have not hesitated to do so. At the time of the Bolshevik revolution, the Bolsheviks were about to go bankrupt after succeeding to power when they were bailed out by the bankers. One would think that capitalism and bolshevism would not be compatible, but the capitalists like socialism, because they can control a socialist government by controlling the men at the top. They have been working continuously to socialize America, and are succeeding, step by step. At the present time, about half the people are being supported by government checks, and losing their freedoms meanwhile. Things to look out for in the creeping trend to socialism are: concentration of power in the administrative branch of government (the president, his cabinet and the powerful bureaucracies), confiscation of firearms, restrictions on free movement from place to place, and restrictions on the flow of capital.

Men play out their dramas of trickery, intrigue and evil at all levels of government and business activity, from top to bottom, The Brotherhoods have said that men and governments have gone past the point of no return, and there is no way they can redeem themselves or erase their negative karmic imbalance. Therefore the only solution is to start over with a new civilization, the coming Kingdom of God.

Chapter Eight
Creation

The information contained in this chapter is taken with permission, from the book, The Ultimate Frontier, *by Eklal Kueshana, published by The Stelle Group. Most of it consists of direct quotations from the book, although paragraphs at the beginning and end of the chapter have been shortened without altering the meaning of the text.*

Creation of life on Earth was the work of Angels from the fifth plane of existence, or Angelic Plane, under the direction of Jehovah. There is still another plane of existence between the Angels and God; the Archangelic Plane, and above it is the Celestial Plane. The seven planes of existence, then, are the Physical, Etheric, Astral, Mental, Angelic, Archangelic and Celestial. The atoms composing them are similar on each plane, except for the nutation rate, which is one octave higher than that of the atoms in the plane below it. The Archangelic Plane is presided over by Melchizedek, who is the Christ that appeared on Earth.

Our Vital bodies are a function of the Etheric Plane, and in the same way all animal and plant life, and all other matter, down to the atoms composing it, have Vital "bodies" or frameworks impressed into the ether. The mind has a special effect on the ether, and the more intense our thoughts are, the greater is the effect. Those Egos living in the fourth plane of existence, the Mental Plane, are able to precipitate matter directly from the ether by building a mental pattern of the object step by step in infinite detail, and then completing this etheric pattern with physical substance. The object so created will be in every way as durable, serviceable and otherwise similar to the same object created by physical means. The precipitation of objects directly from the ether would not be easy for us on the Physical Plane, but we can precipitate material things which we desire intensely and on which we concentrate our thoughts, because the thoughts generate impulses which attract conditions favorable to the achievement of our desires. If we use every legitimate means possible, with determination and a positive attitude, the material things we need and want will come to us. Also, remember and use the power of prayer, which can literally work miracles. It is always available, ready to help you.

The universe is ordered by intellect, in every phase, and without Angelic or Archangelic thought to sustain it, the Physical Plane would not exist. The mind is distinct from the brain, which is functional only on the Physical Plane. Mind is a power given only by God and made part of the human Ego.

The following information has come from the Angelic Host to the Masters and Adepts. It begins about seven billion years ago, on another planet which we shall call Klarian. The inhabitants of this planet had reached such a state of perfection that most of them were Masters, and they found little use for their advanced technology, as they could precipitate their needs directly. After a few thousand years more, all those who had attained Mastership advanced, along with all the other Masters on all other planets, to the Angelic Plane. The ones left behind were stripped of all knowledge gained, and returned to the Celestial Host to be held in abeyance. The Egos of the Angelic Plane were advanced to the Archangelic Plane, and the planet Klarian was then dissolved into nothingness. The Archangels moved up to the Celestial Plane, and dissolved the sun around which the planet Klarian had revolved. The same was done throughout the universe, so that all the stars and attendant planets ceased to exist. Time, because it is a function of matter on the Physical Plane, came to an end.

This great event, which occurs every several billion years, is known as the Progression of the Life Wave. All is still and void on the Physical Plane, because it has ceased to exist. But on the Angelic, Archangelic and Celestial Planes there is much activity: training and planning for a new creation. When all was in readiness, Creation began. First, the Archangels created the stars, and time began again. Around these stars, the Angelic Host created planets from great gaseous clouds, and on each of these man evolved. The Christ, who was one of the Angelic Host when Klarian was evolved, is now Regent of the Archangelic Host, which created our Sun, and this is the reason He is sometimes referred to as "The Day Star On High." Jehovah, who was human on the planet Klarian, was elected Regent by the Angelic Host. Each of the planets has its own Angelic Host, and life apparently flourishes on each of our sister planets. Though physical attributes may differ on each planet in order to adapt to conditions there, the qualities of love, kindliness and faith are the same everywhere.

(Author's note: I personally do not believe there is human life similar to ours on any other planet in our Solar System, from the scientific information available at the present time. I notice the author of *The Ultimate Frontier* uses the words "apparently" and "may be" to qualify his statements, so this is probably not a quotation from the Angelic Host. There could very well be human life on a higher plane of existence on each of the planets, but life in the Physical Plane would need to be radically different on any of the planets we know anything about).

As our planet cooled, vast steam clouds condensed and rocks solidified into land masses. The clouds fell as rain, and one day the light shone through them. The stage was now set for the Angels to create life. They started with one-celled plants and animals, which later evolved into more complex forms. All the forms that They experimented with were constructed in order to form self-perpetuating species incorporating certain metabolic processes whose genetic pattern would eventually develop into a perfect human being. It was on a certain island that the most promising human form developed, and it was endowed with Mind. Mind, that great power of the fourth plane of existence. Mind was individualized by God, and linked to the physical vehicle by Angels. Other strains of human forms were made extinct at this time. After man was endowed with Mind, no further manipulation of his development was allowed by the Angels. This explains why man's form has remained essentially the same through the ages, while other mammalian forms have changed radically. The Angels continued to develop other animal species, for the benefit of mankind. Man has learned to hybridize certain plants and animals, thus speeding up nature's processes, but new species cannot be created, except by Angels; man was endowed with Mind about one million years ago, so he has been a long time in development to the present stage.

The Earth is far behind other planets in its Egoic development, and the number of Egos who have reached the level of Mastership is smaller than elsewhere. Since all Masters must advance to the Angelic Plane at the same time, those on other planets have been waiting for Earth to catch up, so to speak. In about seven thousand years, those who are unable to advance to Mastership will have to be abandoned.

However, under favorable conditions it is possible for Egos to achieve Mastership in a few incarnations. But the present environment is not conducive to rapid development. This is one of the reasons that the City of Stelle, mentioned earlier, was founded: to provide an environment where Egos can develop and advance toward Mastership. In the new Kingdom of God, there will be every opportunity to achieve rapid Egoic growth. All the inventions and technology necessary will be supplied, and Christ Himself will be the overseer of this new nation.

Chapter Nine
Doomsday

The information contained in this chapter is also taken, with permission, from The Ultimate Frontier *by Eklal Kueshana, published by The Stelle Group.*

We have outlined a calendar of events for the period of the Tribulations, Armageddon and Doomsday, the Great Cataclysm or Judgment Day, and later the establishment of a new nation on the continent which is to rise in the Pacific Ocean. Following is a description from the Brotherhoods of the geological and astronomical explanation for the cataclysm and its effect on the world.

The rising out of the sea of the new continent of Mu is of such importance that the Bible has many references to it. The mechanics by which this will occur follows the same geologic pattern as has been the case in the long geologic history of our world. The Earth's crust is continually in the process of rising and falling, becoming ocean and continent, and producing the stratified layers evident in mountainous areas. Our planet's surface rocks, which are about 30 miles thick at most, float upon the denser underlayment. The underlayment is subjected to such extreme heat and pressure that it cannot crystallize, and although it is essentially solid material, it does not have the underlying crystalline structure to give it dimensional stability. It is very much like a rubbery plastic, and comprises the intermediate layer buffering the hard rock surface from the liquid core of the planet.

You may already know that Greenland was once a tropical island, although it is now mostly covered by glacial ice. The last major shift in the Earth's land masses occurred with the sinking of Mu 26,000 years ago. The Earth doesn't change its axis, because the whirling molten core gives it gyroscopic stability. However, our planet's crust slid several thousand miles to reach a tenable equilibrium which it had lacked before it shifted. The shift was started by ever-widening glaciers in the vast, thick polar ice, accumulated in a lop-sided deposit on the spinning surface of the planet. The weight of the inconceivable tonnage of these glaciers, and the resulting imbalance, was sufficient to cause severe centrifugal aberrations in the Earth's rotation, which literally shook the foundations of the continents.

Although the ice was the major contributor, other factors also contributed to the Earth's instability. The Earth is constantly undergoing a shrinkage in overall size, and since the rigid crust cannot conform to this change in dimension, as readily as the liquid core, the crust must adjust itself by a settling process that makes itself known by earthquakes. The faults produced by the settling process permit rocks, at a depth of about 15 miles, to liquify as pressure is relieved. The molten rock wells up through the faults, and can shoot out over large areas, to considerable depth. For about a thousand years prior to the sinking of Mu, this type of activity was prevalent and was particularly extensive along the southeast coast of Mu, near where Easter Island is presently located. Continuous arches were also thrust up by the settling action, which allowed the crust to rest more commodiously on the plastic layer. As time went on, the whole surface structure became shot through with a maze of cracks and pockets, and when the polar ice caps began to slide, the Earth's surface began to break up and move over the plastic underlayment. The principal movement was completed within about 72 hours, but relatively minor adjustments continued for several centuries. New mountain ranges were thrust up, and continents were depressed or elevated. Oceans were displaced, and almost everything was changed, seemingly overnight.

The same situation is evolving in the world today. The crust is again out of a state of equilibrium, the continental arches are ripe for buckling, and the ice packs, while much smaller, are unbalanced. The trigger this time, however, will be from an outside source. On May 5th of the year 2000 A.D. the planets of the Solar System will be arranged in almost a straight line in space. Our planet will be subjected to enough gravitational distortion to trip the delicate balance. Although one cannot normally expect mere planetary configuration to have such a great effect, many factors within our Earth are joining to produce instability around the turn of the century. The developing state of the Earth's structure, and the effect that the other planets will have upon it was long ago carefully measured and analyzed by the Masters, who, with the aid of Melchizedek, arranged Their program for the establishment of the Kingdom of God to coincide with this horrendous cataclysm. The Book of Revelation is mostly concerned with this period. It foretells events leading to the turn of the century. During the period which begins after 1953, which is the start of the Aquarian Age, changes in the climate will be noted all over the world. Meteorological upheavals will give rise to destructive winds, floods, draught and a generally high incidence of disruptive conditions (see Rev. 16: 1-13). The final battle of Armageddon is then recounted, and the chapter finishes with a description of the cataclysmic earthquakes and volcanic eruptions which shortly follow Armageddon.

The viciousness and hatefulness of the battle of Armageddon will reach new lows. The weapons for it are being forged at this very moment. The period of Armageddon began in 1914 with World War I, and will continue with progressively bigger and more destructive wars. The battle of Armageddon will be the culmination of this series of violent outbursts. The last war will begin in 1998, and will end in wholesale obliteration in November, 1999. A few months later the seismic reapportionment of most of the land masses of the Earth's crust will come upon the survivors of Armageddon as a blessing. After Armageddon and Doomsday, less than one-tenth of the world's population will be alive to see the year 2001.

The intensity of the earthquakes will be greater than has ever been measured by scientists. All the volcanoes in the world will burst forth, and a host of new ones will join them. Vast quantities of heavy gases, like carbon dioxide and sulfur dioxide, will be hurled into the air by the erupting volcanoes. The gases will become super-cooled in the upper reaches of the atmosphere, and then descend upon the surface of the Earth in convection currents of such magnitude that hurricane winds will howl over the surface of the world. The skies will be filled with dust and choking fumes, so that even the sun will not be seen for months. Walls of water a thousand feet high will roll across the submerging lands and sweep away everything before them. Sea and land animals, vegetation, silt and sand will be shredded into jumbled muck. Where soil is not washed away, it will be covered by boulders and stones, and the newly-exposed sea bottom will be useless for growing crops. The stench of decay and the bleak destruction everywhere will drive many human survivors hopelessly insane. Those who have the strength of their convictions will rebuild their civilization and the world. Those people, of course, will comprise the Kingdom of God, and they will be brought through the awful destruction soon to be visited upon the world.

Doomsday will not be without its advantages, for it will usher in the Golden Age. After October, 2001 A.D., the Kingdom of God will be formed. The karmic indebtedness of mankind as a whole will be taken care of to a great extent by these occurences. In Revelation it is promised that evil will be bound, which is to say that the influence of the Black Mentalists on the people who survive will be restrained. On the Judgment Day, all those who are pure in heart will be spared. The careless and the thoughtless will be removed. The selection will be made on Egoic advancement and personal karmic balance. The Kingdom of God must have no karma at its inception, therefore each individual must carry none into the new nation. Let these warnings be heeded by those who can comprehend.

In 533 A.D. Dionysius proposed that the calendar year be counted from the birth of Christ instead of the founding of Rome. His researches indicated that Christ was born during the 28th year of the reign of Augustus Caesar. But here is where the Brotherhoods interfered with Dionysius' reckoning. He failed to uncover the fact that Augustus reigned for four years under his own name, Octavian, before he was named Augustus by the Roman Senate. The Brotherhoods know that Jesus was born on October 4th, 4 B.C., but it would have been awkward for Doomsday to fall in the year 2004 A.D., since certain properties make 2000 A.D. the preferred year. The time of the great earthquakes has not been brought about by higher intelligence, but is merely the natural result of geophysical forces. However, it suits the purposes of the Brotherhoods to make their plans for mankind coincide with this scientifically predictable cataclysm. When the world has become quiescent again and the new nation is established, there will be a period of peace and tranquility such as no nation has previously enjoyed on this planet. After about ten centuries, Christ will come again as Melchizedek, and use a physical body precipitated from basic substance, just as He did when He became the first emperor of Lemuria. He will reign for another 1000 years, and since all evil influences will have been eliminated, all Egos will have an opportunity to advance to Mastership.

Chapter Ten
The Important Things In Life

Information contained in this chapter was also taken, with permission, from The Ultimate Frontier *by Eklal Kueshana.*

I once thought it was of little use to spend a lifetime acquiring knowledge and experience, skills and character, only to have it all go down the drain when one dies. Now I know that all this accumulated knowledge is not wasted at all, because it goes with the Ego to the Astral Plane to add to his store of knowledge and experience already acquired in past incarnations. This uplift in character will be apparent when the Ego selects a vehicle for his next incarnation. He, or she, will be able to incarnate into a higher level and more likable environment more suitable to further advancement.

The Black Mentalists have been mentioned earlier, and they have such a profound effect on our lives that it is worthwhile to know more about them. Since very early days the priests and medicine men have wielded great power over the people, and many were corrupt, giving the people false ideas for their own ends, many of which are with us to this day as common beliefs. In the early Egyptian period they ruled the Pharaohs by terrorizing them with non-existent gods which they invented. They also invented the concept of using the physical body in later lifetimes in order to reap the enormous profits from embalming. Later the priests were discredited by one of the Pharaohs who came into power about 1375 B.C. His name was Akhnaton. He made many reforms in government and in the peoples' way of life. He also made reforms in religion, and began the practice of worshiping one god. Akhnaton was murdered by the priests, but his work had done much to advance the cause of civilization. The priests were clever, shrewd, and mentally developed to the point where they practiced clairvoyance and mental telepathy. They also had the ability to read others' thoughts, so they were always able to be ahead of their enemies in their nefarious plans. They were organized as Black Mentalists, and they are still with us today. It is man's negative attitude toward life that gives the Black Mentalists the opportunity to move in. They are always ready to dominate the minds of men, and to use them for their own evil ends. But a man who is thinking positively, who is bright and cheerful and optimistic toward life, with love and joy in his heart, is then attuned to Christ, and Christ functions through him, by sympathetic attraction. But when a man is fearful, hateful and without hope, then he is naturally attuned to the forces of evil, and evil forces function through him. Since man has a negative outlook acquired through thousands of incarnations when he had a brutal struggle for survival, he is an easy prey for those seeking to influence his mind.

The Black Mentalists, through mass hypnosis, are also able to influence and impose their wills on whole groups of people telepathically. I imagine this is responsible for the conduct of some mobs and rioters. The Black Mentalists are strictly human Egos, and there is no such thing as the devil or fallen Angels. Anyone can neutralize the mind-boggling effect of a Black Mentalist at any time by simply asking Christ for help. The difficulty is in recognizing the evil influence for what it is, as the Mentalists are able to use every disguise and camouflage, and every ruse and trick to achieve their purposes. Man seems to be totally unaware of the tremendous mental power inherent in him for good, which if exercised, could raise the world out of its present state and on the road to Egoic advancement and happiness. We must be on guard at all times against our minds being swayed by Black Mentalists, and we must pray to Christ for help in warding them off. An individual who is not a Master is no match for them. Most ordinary Egos are not bothered by the Mentalists unless they show an interest in Egoic advancement, but the Mentalists do not want anyone to reject their enticements and mind-twisting, because it would put them out of buisness forever.

Men are free to choose between good and evil, and they will not be influenced in their decisions by Christ or the Brotherhoods. If they turn toward the good way of life, they will be helped — but only if they ask for help. This is the reason it is essential to pray. The power of the Brotherhoods is far greater than that of the Black Mentalists, but the Brotherhoods cannot interfere in one's life except by specific request. And this is why there is no Guardian Angel hovering over us to keep us out of trouble. Man must advance through his own efforts, and must experience negative emotions and events in order to learn and obtain knowledge. Man has always been slow to take advice or to learn from the experience of others, and must learn everything the hard way, by his own trial and error.

One thing in particular an Ego should be on guard against, is allowing anyone to influence his mind, whether by hypnotism, or whatever means. As an example, it is possible for an Ego from the lower Astral Plane to enter a physical body if the mind is not in full control at the time. Something like this happens in cases of schizophrenia, or dual personality.

What is sin? It is any thought or action by a human being which eventually has results that are not for the good of all persons concerned. Note that thoughts are included with actions, because thoughts are preliminary to action, and also because of the power of thought on the environment.

Persons who use tobacco, alcohol or narcotics suffer a hormone imbalance which causes an appetite for these drugs. The hormone imbalance is generated by mental stress and neurosis. The very real physiological need for these stimulants cannot be overcome on the physical level. One's endocrine glands are influenced by the Vital Body, which is on the second plane of existence. The Vital Body readily responds to the Ego's mental activities. Emotional tensions and upsets produce a corresponding imbalance in the Vital Body, and soon thereafter in the endocrines. Only spiritual peace, plus mental and emotional well-being, can reverse this hunger for detrimental chemicals. Those persons who drink for intoxication impair their brain and spinal centers, which are important to Egoic perfection. A single drunkard or dope addict may be a small loss to Christ's great work, for the emotional perversion which led the person to use these drugs are themselves contrary to the mental attunement demanded for Egoic advancement.

It is important to learn to discern what causes the good and bad conditions operating in your life, and this requires alert observation and rational analysis. Life is a great teacher, and we have many examples provided for us. Fortunately we do not need to suffer from these things, which can be learned from careful observation of the misfortunes of others. Every occurrence in the world is the result of a thought or deed. One must learn the proper actions to put into operation, so that the environment will be more to his liking. One's environment is the result of his own thoughts and actions. He and he alone is responsible for everything he enjoys and suffers in this life. Everyone has the power of mental precipitation, and uses it daily, whether he knows it or not. The things we think about most, become those which tend to enter our environment. To concentrate upon fear, disease and disaster will eventually bring them to pass. To desire a greater income will give rise to ideas, to a plan of action, and to sources of income. To have a mental attitude of confidence gives rise to undaunted living. To fear calamities brings one to only the gloomy aspects of everything, and — lo and behold! — calamity dogs at one's heels. Bargain with life for a penny, and a penny and no more than a penny, will be acquired. If one unwaveringly believes life will bring him health, happiness and prosperity, then these become manifest in his life, for such is the power of mental energy over the physical plane of existence.

Precipitation is a fact, which when one unconsciously uses it regularly, becomes a firm belief and practical tool. One's so-called "'luck" is the result of his karmic account carried over from past incarnations, and also of his conduct during the earlier years of his current lifetime. The thoughts put into action by an individual come back to him in kind, and in similar intensity. Kindness shown to others returns as a kindly environment. A smiling demeanor elicits smiles from others. A gloomy disposition promotes a growl from others. Consideration to others brings consideration from others. Selfish grasping results in loss of what one grabs. If one sows the seeds of hate, lust or brutality, he shall reap a life full of these same things directed against him.

Past and present thoughts and actions account in every detail for the Ego's present environment. No one else has determined it; even the body one inhabits was chosen solely by the Ego before the egg was impregnated. And the civilization into which one has incarnated was earned by past effort. If you want your environment to improve, merely uplift the quality of the thoughts on which you concentrate. Initiate the actions toward others which you would have them show toward you. Perform excess services, in order that your karma may improve. Make the Twelve Great Virtues a part of your life, and ingrain them deeply into your soul. They are: *tolerance, patience, forbearance, kindliness, sincerity, humility, devotion, charity, courage, precision, efficiency and discrimination.*

If your personality is not what you would like it to be, then change your attitudes. Your personality today is the result of your reactions to all the experiences you have ever had. Inasmuch as you today are the result of yesterday's thinking, the person you will be tomorrow is determined by what you think today. Aim your thoughts toward the person you seek to become, and the years will see your desire come to pass. It is you alone who controls the nature of the thoughts flowing through your mind. If negative thoughts crop up, do not pursue them; replace them with positive thoughts instantly. Do not dwell on hateful, fearful or lustful contemplation. Consciously switch to thoughts of a creative project, pleasant memories, love of Christ, vacation plans or some other idea. After all, it's *your* mind, and *you* control what is passing through it. Carefully select the quality of the thoughts on which you contemplate, for your thoughts have direct action on your personality and your environment. Hoping that the good things of life will enter one's environment, but fearing all the while that they may not, will surely result in failure to secure the desired good, for fear and lack of confidence will result in failure of precipitation. Faith is the antithesis of fear, and to obtain a firm faith, one has only to test the principles of universal law, to see that they always work. Faith is the unshakable knowledge that God's laws never fail. One should have confidence in the essentially benign nature of human existence.

It is a truism of all mankind that there is no such thing as chance. We are always in the right place at the right time. One might be killed as an innocent bystander, wholly blameless in the immediate circumstances, yet no one has ever died an untimely death, or in an unwarranted manner. We may unwittingly find ourselves in the locale of the accidental means of our death, but our work is fulfilled before transition can occur; we are never the victims of chance. Happenings of life are determined by our own previously instituted policies, and never is anything like predestination imposed upon us.

Sex is one of the important things in life, and here is what the Brotherhoods say about it:

Don't let anyone tell you that marital sex is laughable, impure or in any way unworthy of a man. God divided the Human Life Wave into two equal human sexual polarities in order that men and women should be inexorably drawn to one another. There were three major objectives to be accomplished by means of bisexual attraction. The first is the most obvious: procreation of the race. The second puspose was to provide a regenerating fount for men and women. Sexual orgasm releases an occult energy which balances certain elements within the creative makeup of human bodies. Intellectual power and procreative power are the two factors of creative energy. The greater one's Egoic development, the greater his powers of creativity; therefore, the greater one's Egoic advancement, the greater are his intellect and capacity for sex. Intellect and sex counterbalance each other in every Ego. If either factor is used to a much greater extent than the other, mental and spiritual imbalance results. The third purpose of God's creation of sexual polarity is the most important by far: the compelling desire an Ego feels for extensive companionship with a mate is the means for teaching human beings how to get along with at least one other person on an intimate day-by-day basis. After thousands of incarnations of practice and cooperation, the emotions and mutual concerns slowly develop between mates. While man was still in prehistoric times, he began to extend these emotions to family members and his neighbors, and has gradually evolved tribal cooperation and humane considerations.

The social growth that arose from sexual attraction was according to God's intentions. Sexual attraction is much more powerful than people realize. The magnetism that draws men and women together is a force beyond the Physical Plane of existence. Perhaps this accounts for sex being so mysterious and baffling to the scientists. It is a matter of great importance that two Egos of opposite polarity create a neutral balanced entity in the universe, which is a true marriage. Until an Ego is united in such a polar coupling, he feels a vague restless yearning, a dissatisfaction with life, which defies description or analysis. Each Ego is but half of a unit which seeks completion.

Unfortunately, all marriages do not result in a balanced polar coupling. When the respective Egoic advancements of a man and his wife are not equal, the marriage becomes forced, and does not result in polar neutrality. It is sad indeed when a man and a woman join in wedlock merely for the satisfaction of sexual passions, or for convenience, or money reasons and the like. The union will likely be strained for its duration. Since marriage is for a lifetime, it is important that very careful consideration be given to choosing a mate in order that a balanced coupling may result. The fact that Egos incarnate into environments of similar advancement helps to assure the possibility of contact between Egos who would combine to form a neutral polarity.

Chapter Eleven
Life On The Astral Plane

Information contained in this chapter is taken, with permission, from The Ultimate Frontier *by Eklal Kueshana.*

We have learned that when we have done our work here on the Physical Plane, and are ready to leave our physical body and move on to the Astral Plane, it will be a pleasurable new experience in which we are likely to meet old friends and relatives, and live in a bright, cheerful environment that eliminates many of the disenchanting features of our present existence. We will also have an opportunity there to check our karmic account and plan the necessary steps to bring it into balance. But the Astral Plane is not a passport to infinite knowledge.

To be relieved of the physical vehicle does not confer mental attitudes or knowledge not already learned. We, as Egos, are the same after the body dies as we were in physical life. Our heaven or hell is within us, and we mold the nature of our after-life during our life on Earth. Fearful, hateful and spiteful people carry these personality traits into their Astral existence, and thereby fix limitations on the happiness they will experience in the Astral Plane. Their negative emotions attune these Egos with the lower vibratory rate of the lower Astral Plane, which is commonly called hell. There are various levels of hell, from the lowest, where vile Egos and murderers, associated with the Black Mentalists, have bound themselves; to the other end of the spectrum, where dwell the unhappy Egos who dubiously refuse to learn that the mere elevation of the quality of their thoughts can promote them to upper Astral existence.

The lower Astral Plane is confused, dark and dejected. By comparison, the upper Astral Plane is bright, musical and expansive. Egos who are happy, loving, wise and helpful naturally gravitate to the upper Astral Plane on transition. There they may receive instruction from the Higher Beings of our Human Life Wave, in order to become better prepared for future incarnations. But it is only on the Physical Plane that we gain the knowledge that becomes a permanent part of our soul equipment, and this restriction applies until the Ego attains Adeptship. The type of personality and character a person evolves in physical life determines the station he will suffer or enjoy in the Astral Plane. However, after he arrives upon the Astral Plane, at the station corresponding to his character, he can modify his situation there by changing his emotions, thoughts and desires. Character, not acts, determines the status of Egos on the Astral Plane.

The criminal murderer kills because of his depravity, but so may a gentle nurse, by careless or indiscriminate administering of medication to patients. Karmically, both the criminal and the nurse, during later incarnations, must suffer deaths similar to the ones they inflicted. One of them killed by intent, the other by lack of due attention. Karma will settle their accounts on the Physical Plane if they haven't, in the meanwhile, compensated for their hurtful deeds by rendering appropriate excess service to others. If you recall, karma means "carry-over." That is because karmic accounts are ignored on the Astral Plane. The Astral Plane is concerned only with the uplift of an Ego's character, providing he so desires.

The ignorance which binds a man on Earth will also bind him in heaven. But as rapidly as a man uplifts his attitude in heaven, his level of attunement correspondingly rises toward the higher vibrations of the upper Astral Plane. It is a sad commentary on human beings that many sink lower on the Astral Plane while they are there. For example, soldiers who are slain in battle often continue their hateful and vengeful contentions after they arrive on the Astral Plane. The dark emotions they persist in sustaining tear down whatever advancement they have gained in prior lives. Unless these Egos come to a state of forgiveness, peace and serenity, they cannot hope to see upper Astral life.

Attunement to different vibrations does not mean a change in the nutation rate, which is constant within a particular plane of existence, but to vibrations analagous to electromagnetic radiation in the Physical Plane. It is these Astral radiations which afford sympathetic attunement between similar Egos. Just as many classes of society coexist in a large city, so it is in the Astral Plane. The different classes of culture that exist in society may impinge on one another in stores, factories and places of amusement, but the members of any one class seem unable to find much in common with the members of a different class. Socialites, poor slum dwellers, intellectuals, skid-row bums, middle-class Christians, underworld hoodlums, unskilled laborers, and college-educated executives all live together in the same city, and are known to one another, but the mores and customs distinctive to each class seem intolerable for any of the other classes. Analagous to these coexisting worlds within a society, the Astral Plane is likewise compartmentalized. On the Astral Plane, mental precipitation is practically instantaneous; the surroundings in which one finds himself are the direct result of the kind of thoughts he sustains. Egos who share the same level of happiness, serenity, helpfulness and love would naturally be attuned to one another and would be surrounded by the same kind of environment, because similar thoughts determine a correspondingly similar environment. These Egos would find themselves together yet distinct from those above and below their respective levels of advancement.

Each type of emotion has its own characteristic vibrational frequency. When an Ego experiences an emotion, he generates radiated energy upon the third plane of existence. This vibratory energy is radiated whether the Ego is residing in the Astral Plane, or is incarnated in a physical body. The clairvoyant person actually sees these vibrations as colored auras enveloping the Ego's Astral body. Each character trait and emotion is definitely related to an Astral radiation of a specific color. Love is at the highest end of the Astral vibrational spectrum, and exhibits a clear violet color in an Ego's aura. Hate is at the lower end of the spectrum, and is indicated in an Ego's character by a murky red in the Astral aura. Because almost everyone, at any given moment, possesses all the shades possible to any human character, each in a varying degree of refinement, he simultaneously exhibits the whole spectrum of color vibrations. The amplitude or intensity of each vibrational frequency — that is, the relative brightness of each color in the Astral aura — is determined by the extent to which the Ego has developed the corresponding characteristic or emotion. Love and hatred, for instance, may easily coexist in an Ego's makeup. He may profoundly love Christ and all mankind, and because of his supreme refinement, the amplitude of his love frequency will be intense and dominant in his emotional spectrum. But he may also suffer great hatred and fear of the Black Mentalists. This negative emotion will also appear in his Egoic aura, in proportion to the intensity of his hatred and fear. You may say that hatred and fear of the Black Mentalists is fitting and proper, but it is not. The Ego's hatred does not hurt the Black Mentalists, it only holds down the overall level of refinement of the Ego doing the hating. That is why Christ commanded us to love our enemies, because such love enhances one's Egoic advancement. Indeed, Christ loves even the evil Black Mentalists. They are human beings, struggling in darkness along the path toward unity with God. Their perverse and negative attitudes are truly pitiful.

The Angels and Archangels are without hatred. Were they to hate, think how disastrous such emotions — charged by their highly advanced powers of precipitation — would be to our universe. Angels are, and must be, the embodiment of loving patience and compassion. A human being's overall spiritual advancement can be measured by averaging the amplitudes of each of the Ego's vibratory frequencies. An Ego is highly advanced when his positive emotions are of intense amplitude. His overall spiritual development determines the quality of his Astral companions, and the level he will occupy in heaven or hell. An Ego resting on the Astral Plane, who plans to re-incarnate, must be of spiritual advancement equal to or exceeding that of the average of the two parents of his proposed new physical vehicle. In this way, no parents suffer a child of lower spiritual advancement than themselves. This is guaranteed by Cosmic Law.

Chapter Twelve
A Sound Body and Mind*

Spiritual stability and harmony demand a sound body and mind. A sound mind cannot exist within an unsound body, and neither can a sound body develop with a distraught mind. The body needs good natural food, as it cannot maintain its health without the raw materials to build on. Exercise is also essential to maintain a vigorous, healthy body. The human body was designed to stand tremendous strain, but one must use good sense to enable it to do so. Respect it for what it is; you are not superhuman. But it is possible to keep your body alive for a hundred years or so. If a person has a sufficient knowledge of human physiology, and the ability to precipitate effectively, he can, according to the teachings of the Brotherhoods, preserve his physical vehicle indefinitely. The normal body has a built-in aging mechanism, so that a lifetime lasts only long enough for the average Ego to derive the optimum benefit from an incarnation. This aging mechanism can be overcome by an advanced mentality, so that balance between the catabolic and anabolic forces of the body's cells can be maintained for prolonged periods without the disadvantages of decrepitude. So long as the vital body on the etheric plane is integral, the physical body

---

*Information contained in this chapter was taken, with permission, from *The Ultimate Frontier* by Eklal Kueshana (The Stelle Group, Stelle Illinois, Cabery P.O. 60919).

can go on and on. Everything necessary for this can be provided by the body itself, provided that ample wholesome food is ingested. The key to longevity is mental precipitation and contemplation upon certain centers within one's body. Adepts, should they need to incarnate, can maintain vigorous life for several hundred years, and those Masters who have chosen to work directly on the Physical Plane with mankind can sustain their bodies indefinitely.

There is no secret formula for longevity, but it is mostly a matter of many sensible little practices, as mentioned earlier. Moderation in all things and maintaining a sunny and youthful attitude is perhaps the best advice for those who are not yet Adepts. The elimination of the harmful waste products of bacteria from within the body is a very effective process for forestalling the aging process, as well. It is understandably impossible to completely eliminate bacteria from our bodies. But if a person maintains a habit of daily bowel evacuation, the principle source of bacterial toxins is removed. The colon's function is to remove moisture from feces, and the longer the waste products remain in the colon, the more the deleterious substances of bacterial decomposition are absorbed into one's blood. The stool should be light in color when eliminated, for the darker it is, the longer it has been stored in the bowel. Another big source of microbial toxins is the coating on the tongue. This should be brushed off with a toothbrush every morning, and rinsed out with water.

Be wary of food fadism. To maintain either a strict and limited vegetarian or meat diet is destructive to the body, and eventually results in mental aberrations which are not conducive to spiritual advancement. Man needs the nutrients in both vegetables and meat; the body is designed to digest both. There is absolutely no spiritual value inherent in one food over another food. To abstain from meat in one's diet because it has base animal vibrations, which might lower the aggregate vibrations of the human vehicle, is outright nonsense. No one ever ate his way to heaven, or to hell either for that matter. Admittedly, the optimum proportion of meat to vegetables in any one individual's diet is different from any one else's. This proportion is each person's responsibility to discover for himself through trial and error. Never try to impose your ideas of diet on another; what is beneficial to your system may be deadly to his.

Sunlight has biological effects not only on plants, but on birds, animals and humans. We already know something of its effect on our skin, but research has found that there is a photo-receptor mechanism in the retina of the eye, that has nothing to do with vision, but is linked to neuro-chemical channels in the pituitary and pineal glands, and other areas of the brain that control the entire endocrine system. These exercise control over the production and release of hormones that control body chemistry, along with nutrition and other factors. Wearing glasses, sunglasses or contact lenses filters out the high-frequency end of the spectrum, which contains the ultra-violet light, so one does not get the benefit of true natural sunlight. This effect is also true of any glass, such as window glass or automobile glass. Of course, too much sun can be harmful, too, but man has evolved in sunlight, and a certain amount seems necessary for his good health. There are now on the market both incandescent and flourescent lights which approximate the light given off by the sun, and it has been found that students studying under these lights do better work than when using ordinary types of lights. In tests with mice, it was found that mice living under sunlight light fixtures had about twice the life span of mice living under conventional artificial light, and also had only half as many tumors. Could this have some significance in relation to the great increase in cancer among humans compared to previous generations who lived more in the outdoors? These tests were conducted at seven different locations by seven different researchers, and the results sent to the

National Cancer Institute and to the American Cancer Society. Both agencies brushed them aside, and continued their twenty-year-long search for a cancer virus, which may or may not exist. A book describing the acitivities of these two agencies and the Food and Drug Administration is worth reading. It is called *World Without Cancer*, by Griffin.

Sophistication, cynicism, and a fear of being thought gullible cause many Egos to reject truth when it comes their way. There are so many cults, religions and 'isms' fostered by charlatans for their own profit that thinking persons tend to reject all unusual information of an occult nature. However, the truly discriminating intellect will weigh and fully investigate all ideas he encounters. Those Egos who have had prior knowledge of truth from previous incarnations will experience an affinity for facts concerning human existence, whenever they happen upon them. Among these are the elect who shall people the Kingdom of God. Even men without spiritual advancement can extend their lives well beyond normal life expectancy by using certain principles of yoga.

Yoga itself is generally not for the occidental personality. Some forms of yoga should be avoided, because of potential hazards. The word yoga means "union." An adherent is called a yogi, and he seeks to achieve simultaneous awareness of three of his four bodies, which function respectively on the Physical, Ethereal and Astral Planes of existence. When he has achieved this end, he is able to perceive happenings on the Ethereal and Astral Planes. Although he may have achieved conscious contact with the higher planes, he is still a long way from functioning in them. His clairvoyant powers are enjoyable and enlightening, but not really conducive to spiritual advancement. A yogic contact with higher planes is not the proper outcome of Egoic refinement, but is a forced experience brought about by physical exercises and excessive breathing exercises. These practices are the disciplines of

Hatha Yoga, which means "union through courage." It is aptly named. The devotee of Hatha Yoga strengthens his body by following an austere esthetic regimen of strenuous exercises and careful diet. To the yogi, his physical vehicle in glorious good health is but the normal starting point for his journey into astral experience. The violent strains to which his body is submitted during the course of his efforts to perceive the great beyond would simply destroy a normal physical vehicle. The yogi subjects the plexuses of his body, which are the control centers of his autonomic nervous system, to many years of a type of mental concentration that is designed to result in conscious control over normally uncontrollable body functions. A practiced yogi can change the rate of his heartbeat, or stop it. He can mentally induce his endocrine glands to change the levels of hormonal secretion, and he can regulate his digestive processes. By coupling his developed bodily control with certain breathing methods, he causes the plexuses of his physical body to enter a state of imbalanced excitation. The plexuses bear an especially close relationship with one's Astral body, and the strange energies released by the excitation of the plexuses bring about a rapport with the yogi's Astral self. When he is in such a state, he can perceive events in the Astral Plane through the eyes of his Astral body, and the eyes of his Vital body. This is really a mental perception, but can best be expressed by saying "eyes." During this state, he can perceive the life forces emanating from another Ego, and can contact persons residing on the Astral Plane. There are many wondrous experiences to be gained from such glimpses, but the terrifying and dangerous prelude to his paradise hardly makes it worthwhile. According to the teachings of the Brotherhoods, the yogi who forces his way into the higher planes must first encounter the Dweller of the Threshhold of the lower Astral Plane before he can proceed further. The Dweller at the Threshhold is a hideous entity of evil malevolence. Most yogis who struggle to this kind of contact with this kind of Astral existence, are riven by convulsions of sheer terror as they encounter the Dweller. The vile Egos and Black Mentalists at the lower end of the Astral Plane then have a perfect inroad to the defenseless yogi's body and they drive him hopelessly insane. Those rare yogis who have successfully overcome their fright at meeting the Dweller avow that it was an experience that they hope never to go through again.

Chapter Thirteen
Clairvoyance*

Hatha Yoga has something worthwhile to offer only as a means of achieving physical health and vibrant wellbeing. The preferred path to clairvoyance and proper functioning on the Astral Plane while still living in a physical vehicle is through Rajah Yoga, the "Kingly Union." This is essentially the way of the Brotherhoods, and it is proper for the occidental mentality.

No physical exercises or breathing systems are involved. Moreover, it provides maximum protection from the lower Astral entities when the Ego's breakthrough to Astral clairvoyance occurs. This method requires only that one gradually increase the frequency of one's spiritual vibrations through character uplift, emotional refinement, and proper development of virtuous living. This is a relatively slow course, but the one which was followed by all the Great Ones who have achieved Adeptship and Mastership.

Attempted short-cuts to spiritual power almost invariably lead to sorcery: mentalism through enthrallment by the Black Mentalists. The road to spiritual greatness may seem surprisingly simple, but only because it is. Man was intended to rise naturally in smooth sequence from the clod he was at creation to the perfection of Mastership. Attune-

---

*Information contained in this chapter is taken, with permission, from *The Ultimate Frontier* by Eklal Kueshana (The Stelle Group, Stelle Illinois, Cabery P.O. 60919).

ment with Christ's principles, harmless living, karmic balance, and a fervent and burning desire to be a Brother comprise the path to advancement. And of these, perhaps the last is the most important. Living among people and solving the problems of life are essentail to the development of virtue and soul enlargement. The quiet life of contemplation and meditation in an ivory tower existence is a blind alley. To avoid life and situations is merely to delay the mastering of problems and karmic pitfalls which must eventually be disposed of in another lifetime if they are not tackled now. If one runs away from a painful or difficult situation, instead of facing it until it is solved, it will only reappear as a similar situation of even greater difficulty. When a problem is finally solved, it ceases to be a bothersome, distressing thing. Should the same circumstance ever surface again, it is easily disposed of because one has the knowledge and experience to overcome it. Fortunately, no one is ever exposed to a situation he is not able to handle successfully.

To force oneself into realms where one's spiritual advancement and intellectual understanding have not as yet paved the way will inevitably result in contacting Black Mentalists. The deliberate misinformation the Black Mentalists force upon misguided persons seeking voices and visions from heaven are worse than useless. Many persons, especially women, may be spontaneous mediums who hear spirit voices and see ectoplasmic processes. The Brotherhoods' philosophy considers these processes to be inspired by evil forces. Egos of high advancement can contact the higher Astral Plane, and can see and hear the persons with whom they are conversing there, but these persons never disclose their ability to perform such feats of true clairvoyance, except to authorized Brothers. The commercialized clairvoyant, however sincere, is an unwitting tool of evil. The person who consciously seeks such occult powers by deliberate courting of the forces of evil is known as a witch, in the negative sense of the word. The end cost of such an alliance with the Black Mentalists is Egoic enslavement by them, and destruction of soul. To try to push your sense perception beyond the level of your spiritual advancement is folly. The senses naturally become able to perceive the higher planes in direct proportion to achievement of balanced Egoic advancement. No special effort to intensify ones extra-sensory powers is necessary as spiritual advancement is being attained. However, there is a project one can work on now.

In accordance with their present knowledge, psychologists have divided the mind into two classifications, the conscious and the subconscious. This is a fallacy, for no such division actually exists. The apparent barrier against full conscious utilization of all the brain's potential can be dispelled with just one word, *awareness*. Egos who have achieved several degrees of Brotherhood have fully penetrated this so-called barrier. They are exceptionally balanced and serene persons, because they do not suffer phobias, prejudices, fixations, and other personality disturbances brought about by obscure feelings located in the subliminal backreaches of the brain. All the functions of the brain are available to the Advanced Ones. So, if one wishes to embark upon a very worthwhile but harmless exercise, he would work to increase his inner awareness. Self-analysis, astute soul-searching, and meditation on the attitudes forming events in one's early life will tend to penetrate the veil between one's buried past and present consciousness. The vast storage facilities for information within the subconscious mind can also be made available through awareness. Everything one has done, thought and seen in this lifetime is recorded there in infinite detail. Picture the advantages of making such a fund of information readily available! The subconscious possesses fantastic power in mathematical calculating, and it can also be assigned to conveniently govern routine tasks like driving an automobile and performing repetitive operations so one is free to concentrate on more important matters at the same time. Awareness is the key to full use of your brain power.

It is very true that use of the principles of yoga can enable a man to overcome the vibratory phenomena of heat and gravity. Even natives of certain primitive tribes, whose ancient ceremonies require them to walk on burning coals, are able to come away without even a slight burn. This amazing feat has been authenticated by scientists innumerable times, and yet to science the natives' immunity to burns remains a mystery. This seeming miracle is the result of the natives' absolute unwavering faith that it can be done. The fire-walker knows that it can be done, because he has seen his father, brothers and acquaintances do it. Once he himself has done it, no scientist will ever convince him that it is an impossibility to walk on fire unharmed. Thus faith literally works wonders. The medicine men of this tribe cure diseases by the same device. The patients firmly believe the medicine man can cure them with hokus pokus, and Behold! — they are cured.

What faith can cure, it can prevent. The germ theory of disease is incomplete, because it does not take into account mental attitudes of the human being. Fear of disease is a principal factor in its contraction. To have confidence in the fact that one can overcome the adverse influences of microbial infection by means of mentally reinforcing the natural defenses of the body is a force of such magnitude that a positive outlook alone will prevent illness from ever threatening. By the same token, worry over one's health can precipitate susceptibility to sickness. The common cold is a plague because almost everyone is conditioned to accept its inevitability. Scientific investigation has demonstrated that only one cold sufferer out of four actually has an infection to account for the symptoms. The other three are suffering identical symptoms, which merely mimic the true cold. These people were so sure that a momentary stuffiness in the nose or a sneeze was the inescapable prelude to a head cold that they suffered for several days with a false cold. There are many organic diseases which a clairvoyant physician is easily able to perceive as being the result of anxiety, tension, fear, hate and worry. Notable among these are cancer, stomach ulcers, heart trouble, endocrine abnormalities and a vast array of emotional and mental disorders. No germs are involved in such illnesses; rather, they consist of a breakdown of normal bodily functions through the action of continual negative thoughts upon the Vital body.

Further illustrating the power of Mind is the work of a professor and psychologist at one of our universities, who has made a survey of cancer patients, and concluded that a typical victim of cancer is a man or woman who was emotionally upset as a child, but who repressed unpleasant experiences, and had great difficulty in expressing anger, or giving vent to hurt. However, they now consider themselves happy, well-adjusted and capable of coping with life. In particular, women who lived in conflict with their mothers, resented sex, and reluctantly accepted the role of women seemed more likely to have breast cancer.

There is much in the world to attract us away from God's purpose. There is much to distract us from our own inner urgings. So it is necessary to recognize in ourselves what we truly want to experience in life. Paul said it very well to the Phillippians — and he said it at a time when man was every bit as troubled, brutalized and entangled in the webs of glamour, purposelessness and conflict as we are today. Paul said, "All that is true, all that is noble, all that is just and pure, all that is lovable and gracious, whatsoever is excellent and admirable — fill all your thoughts with these things."

The practice of the Twelve Great Virtues enumerated by the Brotherhoods is recommended by them for self-advancement, to be used in one's daily life. They are worth repeating: *tolerance, patience, kindliness, forbearance, charity, humility, devotion, sincerity, courage, precision, efficiency and discrimination.* Personal acquistion of the Great Virtues builds character, integrity and morality, and results naturally in the intensification of extra-sensory perception, which affords a direct channel to Higher Sources. Putting these concepts into actual practice is a slow and sometimes exasperating remaking of one's self, but it is the Pathway to Perfection, and you can do it.

What we are is God's gift to us. What we become is our gift to God.

PART TWO
The Power of Love

Chapter Fourteen
How the Brain Develops*

The following chapters deal with the tremendous power of love. Since love is a function of the fourth (or mental) plane of existence, in which we have transcended our physical bodies, and Mind is essentially our way of life on that plane, let us examine more closely the qualities of Mind on the physical plane.

Mind is of the spirit, not the physical body, but it is closely interlocked with our physical brain, and controls it in all the body's functions, both voluntary and involuntary. We know that our thoughts initiate various reactions in our bodies, and every action of our body requires thought to start it. We may not even be conscious of the thought — it may come from our subconscious, the vast storehouse of information collected by the brain over our lifetime, or from the greater storehouse of Mind, which includes every thought, emotion, action and experience in all our many lifetimes up to the present. If it is hard for you to visualize all this, remember that we only have the limited range of our five senses from which to draw conclusions, and we have already learned that there is much more to existence that we do not know about. As Dr. White wrote in *The Ultimate Frontier*, all things will be satisfactorily explained

---

*Information for this chapter was obtained, with permission, from an article published in The Stelle Letter, volume 13, number 8, entitled "The Development of the Human Brain," by Richard Kieninger, published by The Stelle Group, Stelle, Illinois, 60919.

in due time. We are simply not ready to understand the great mysteries of the universe, since our physical brains must rationalize information before accepting it. Physicians are realizing more and more the importance of a cheerful, positive mental attitude, in order for patients to speed their recovery from illness or disease. To this can be added the power of prayer, in which our thoughts go out to reinforce and augment the healing forces of nature. Conversely, a person who does not want to get well, or who has given up fighting for survival, is more likely not to survive. All the negative emotions such as anger, hate, fear and anxiety are harmful to the body in a physical as well as a spiritual way. Living a serene, calm, peaceful existence and avoiding the negativity is the secret to happiness and long life. Remember, it is not what you have, what you are or what you do that makes you happy or unhappy — it is how you feel and believe that is important to you. Think only of good — reject all evil, for it does not exist except in the minds of men.

All of us are busily playing out our little dramas of life, groping for knowledge and spiritual satisfaction, and advancing our Egoic development, whether we realize it or not — for through failure we gain experience to help us in future encounters with life. This is how Mind develops from clod to God. When we are able to look at situations in the light of gaining valuable experience and knowledge rather than simply as success or failure, we are not so likely to be disheartened by disappointments. Then we can analyze our mistakes with a clear head and figure out a plan for the next attempt.

As we grow up and mature, our brain cells are constantly recording new stimuli, adding to our intelligence. Our reasoning power makes use of not only current data, but also whatever storehouse of information is available, already recorded from past experiences. A section of the brain analyzes, compares and decides whether to add it on to present information or to revise the information in light of the new experience. This process never stops, and the more activity we give it, the more it thrives and develops.

A healthy brain and a healthy body go together, and each helps the other. One drink of liquor can kill 200,000 brain cells, and a night of drinking and drunkenness can kill millions of them. Alcohol is a poison, and is harmful to many organs besides the brain. The same goes for tobacco, although they are both so common that we do not think of them as poisons. But give a small boy a few puffs on a cigar, and see how quickly he becomes sick! I know, because I have tried it. If you want to preserve what is left of your intelligence (almost everyone has some brain damage) avoid all substances that are harmful to your body. A prominent doctor says that one of the worst drugs we Americans are addicted to is sugar. It causes all kinds of trouble with our bodies, and is indulged in by young and old alike, by the millions. Some breakfast foods advertised for the kids market contain more than fifty percent sugar. Other drugs, from tranquilizers and marijuana to cocaine and heroin, all cause devastation to our bodies in varying degrees. No amount of talking does any good for the people addicted to these health-robbing substances, until they are ready to quit of their own accord, after they have had the experience of personally testing it for themselves, to their sorrow. The trouble is, after one has gone the route, it is too late to retrieve the damaged brain cells lost in the process.

The brain develops in four stages, in a manner similar to the way it developed during the process of evolution. First the medulla develops — the part at the end of the spinal cord. Then another part develops, called the pons. The midbrain then encloses these two, and finally the part we usually think of as being the brain — the cortex — develops. If these units are not developed in proper order, the one bypassed may not develop properly or fully, and this can also hamper development of higher levels of brain tissue. If proper development has not occurred, one can go back and provide sufficient stimuli to the bypassed part of the brain, and work up again from there. Since no one has ever attained full development of his cortex, there is always a great deal of room for development.

The development of a child's brain depends on many factors, and none of these factors is realized at maximum efficiency in real life. When a child is born, the supply of oxygen to its brain cells is supplied by the umbilical cord, and if this is cut too soon, its brain will suffer from inadequate oxygen supply. The child's brain develops in response to stimuli from its observations and activities, and in order for it to develop, the cells must be near a blood vessel which can supply them with oxygen. Since this condition is never perfect, not all the brain cells are able to develop. Growth of brain cells is also dependent on vitamins, and here again the diet of the child is not perfect, and some brain cells suffer from lack of vitamins and minerals. Although heredity plays some part in child's intelligence, environment is the principal factor in the child's development. A child left in a playpen will not develop as fast as a child left free to crawl on the floor, because the activity of crawling is a necessary part of its training. Even its eyesight is developed in this way. New stimuli affect the child at every stage of its development, and proper stimuli are vital for the maximum development of the child's brain.

So we can see how important it is for the child to have every advantage possible in order to develop his brain from the very moment of birth, and even before birth. A child's brain has pretty well reached its growth by the time he is of school age, so his capacity for learning will be limited by the conditions of his early environment. However, the capacity for genius is in all of us, and the right kind of training can do wonders with even the dullest child. Every child needs experience in coping with the environment, and this experience gives him awareness and intelligence. Children from underprivileged families who are given a change of environment and proper training soon develop into bright, alert scholars with high IQ's. This might seem to be an argument for school integration — however, I think the tendency is to pull bright students down to the level of the slowest, rather than the other way around. I saw recently on a TV program where a black school teacher ran a private school in her home for her own children and those of her neighbors. The results were amazing, not only for the quality of education the students received, but especially for their motivation to learn and to study, which seems to be lacking in our schools today.

I am a firm believer in discipline in the home, and I think if more attention were given to this, it would help solve many of our problems in the schools. If a mother gave her child more personal attention and tutoring right from the start, with the opportunity for real-life experience in growth and understanding, the child would probably be able to do much better after entering school. At least that is the concensus of many learned opinions.

At The Stelle Group in Stelle, Illinois, a school is operated on a system quite different from that used in our public schools. School begins for these children at age two, with their mothers in attendance as well as the children, who have been properly trained by their mothers since birth. They are able to read and write, do mathematical problems and have a general education equal to about the third grade level by the time they are four years old. One mother remarked that there was no limit to her child's ability to learn. Apparently they must be doing things right.

If we assume that our purpose in life is to advance our Egoic or spiritual development with each generation, so that eventually we can achieve true happiness in "heaven," or the astral plane, then our main concern here on earth in the physical plane should be to rear our children to the best of our ability. That does not mean letting kids run wild on their own while the mother is working on a job, sitting in a bar, or otherwise neglecting them. It means planning her life so she can give her children proper attention and care, and educating them and training them for the life experiences that are to follow. It means a return to the concept of the closely-knit family, where kids have the benefit of a mother's love clearly demonstrated by the mother's actions, and reciprocated by the children.

Being a young child's teacher is no easy task, and mothers need training in proper methods and procedures in order to have the best results. At Stelle, mothers are given instruction at meetings and discussion sessions, and also attend seminars at the Better Babies Institute in Philadelphia. Here they become better acquainted with the enormous capacity and insatiable desire for learning in babies and young children. They see the results of proper training in the ability of babies to do things which we might think impossible — and it would be impossible for babies brought up under the conditions they normally encounter in most homes. For instance, babies can learn to read before they learn to walk. At age of three they can do addition, subtraction and division of numbers. At six they know as much as the average elementary school graduate. It would seem that some mothers would have trouble keeping up with such rapid advancement. Of course, fathers are not exempt from this training of their children, and they must also keep abreast of their child's progress, in order for the child to develop into a well-balanced individual, physically, mentally and spiritually. It will certainly be interesting to see what pupils at Stelle are able to attain in life, compared to average students at other schools in the country.

Chapter Fifteen
Mind — Where Love Begins

So far, we have talked mostly about the development of the brain, rather than of the mind. But Mind and brain are closely coordinated in one's Ego, and Mind controls the activities of the brain. When the brain sleeps, it leaves Mind free to leave the physical body temporarily, and to also leave the physical plane of existence if it so desires. Perhaps there is some bit of information it needs about the physical plane, and it can thus obtain it from the Akashic Record on the astral plane, for the record includes all the thoughts, emotions and actions of every entity, or Ego, or soul, from the beginning to the present time. Or perhaps it merely wants to enjoy a change of location for a little while. It must get pretty tired of coping with all the scanning thoughts of our brain during the hours when we are awake!

The ten qualities of Mind are: memory, desire, will, curiosity, consciousness, conscience, creativity, intuition, emotion and reason.*

The mass media have a great effect on the development of our minds. Some effects are good, others are bad. Think of the tremendous impact television has had on our lives, for instance. The effect on the minds of children, who are easily swayed by what they see and hear, can affect their

---

*Reprinted with permission from *The Ultimate Frontier*, by Eklal Kueshana, published by The Stelle Group, Stelle, Illinois 60919.

growth adversely. The media have a great responsibility for the quality and type of material they disseminate to the public, and they do not always assume that responsibility. They accept advertising geared to the subconscious mind rather than to the conscious, to brainwash us into believing their products have merit. They appeal to the sexual emotions of people through all manner of gimmicks, because they know that sex is one of our strongest emotions, and is sure to draw attention.

It has already been mentioned that Mind follows our beliefs rather than the facts. Everyone sees a given situation or condition differently, according to his past experiences and the impressions left on his brain. As the brain evaluates the information available to it, it comes up with an answer, and this varies with each individual. I have been amused during debate to see how two minds can take such widely divergent views of the same topic under debate. As for groups, we have a clear picture of how groups change their positions on political matters from year to year. The communists are masters at brainwashing the masses to make them take slavery and like it. Look at what happened when Castro took over Cuba with only a few hundred men. The events in El Salvador and Nicaragua also demonstrate the effects of a change in group consciousness.

A positive and cheerful outlook works wonders in changing a bad situation into a good one. A problem that looks hopeless to one person may look entirely different to another. A person who sees only negative aspects of a situation, or who allows the negative to overcome the positive, may reject something that would be of great benefit to him, if only he could see the possibilities for positive action on it. It could also happen in reverse, if the person lacks the discrimination to stay out of trouble.

Our emotions are more likely than not to give us a wrong steer. Fear or anxiety can multiply small things into monumental mental blocks — and so can hate and anger.

These four qualities of emotional distress should be eliminated from our thoughts, or at least put into proper perspective so that we can use our reason to overcome them. If we can replace these negative emotions with love, which is positive and is the most powerful emotion of all, then the others fade away and disappear. I am speaking of love for humanity, for one's fellow man, and love for everyone, unconditionally. We will talk more about this later.

Mind and brain are not exactly two separate and distinct parts of the Ego, but are blended together and divided into conscious and subconscious sections. The conscious mind is only the "tip of the iceberg" the part that the brain has decided we should retain for instant recollection. The rest, which is a vast storehouse of all the information, experiences and emotions of our lifetime up to the present, is in the subconscious, and can be drawn on when needed, up to a point.

Although the mind is closely intermingled with the brain, it is not locked into it, but can leave the body and return to it at will during sleep.

When our minds are active, they send out thought impulses which are broadcast through the ether something like radio waves from a transmitter. We do not know exactly how radio or television waves are emitted, but we do know their effects, and have learned how to use these effects to our advantage. Thought waves are apparently very powerful in their effects, as they can be "picked up" thousands of miles away, and will pass through barriers that stop ordinary radio waves. Many experiments have been made along this line, and have shown this to be true. In fact, thought waves can be so powerful in their effects that some highly developed minds are able to precipitate material objects directly from the ether, by intense concentration. These thought waves are electrical in nature, just as everything in our universe is electrical when you get down to the basic subatomic particles that compose it. These particles of matter are actually mere whirling bundles of electrical energy, traveling in orbits so fast that we cannot conceive of them.

Experiments in thought transmission and reception are constantly being carried on by our government and others, and by private organizations, such as Duke University, which has conducted many experiments in ESP and related subjects over the years. The Brotherhoods say that this ability will come naturally to Egos who have developed their minds sufficiently, along with corresponding spiritual advancement.

Learning is accomplished by electrical impulses formed in a network of brain fibers so tiny they can be seen only with an electron microscope. These tiny fibers criss-cross one another, and at the junction where they cross, electrical voltages are built up, and impulses can "jump" from one nerve fiber to another. Each "cell" is like a digital computer component, turning either "on" or "off," or "go — no go," when stimulated by our senses. Just how it results in thought images, emotions and commands to the body for action, and how it radiates thought energy into the ether, is not known — to me, at any rate — and we just have to take it for granted. Scientists are working on this, too, and some day we may have the answers.

We might think of our brain as a tape or wire recorder, where the electrical vibrations are transmitted from the senses directly to the brain cells through the nerve fibers, rather than to a pick-up mechanism as in a tape recorder. We know that the more deeply we concentrate our thoughts on something, the more deeply it is impressed on our brain, and also that repetition causes a deeper impression on the brain each time it is repeated. This is apparent when we try to memorize a poem, an address or phone number or whatever. Also, impressions stick with us better when memorized at an early age, probably because the brain is more easily influenced then. Another curious thing is that children have more ability than adults have to be clairvoyant, use ESP and even communicate with animals. This might be because adults have become more fixed in their ways and in their opinions and beliefs, while children have an open mind to whatever their world has to offer.

One reason that the quality of your thoughts and actions is so important is that all these things are impressed on your subconscious and eventually return to you in the form of physical and mental changes which your body and mind undergo, because of the influence of the subconscious on bodily functions and the mental acceptance of distorted concepts previously encountered. You must be very selective about what you allow to come into your thoughts. The subconscious in not selective. If you think ill of someone, your subconscious takes it as applying to yourself, and as the negative thoughts accumulate, they form a backlog of experience on which your mind diagnoses and compares data, then acts subconsciously to carry out the negative thoughts — on you! A quotation from the Bible is worth repeating, for it is a good thing to remember:

> "All that is true; all that is noble; all that is just and pure; whatever is loveable and gracious; whatever is excellent and admirable; fill all your thoughts with these things."
> —Paul to Philippians 8-4

Now we can see why people can become ill or diseased merely by incorrect thinking. This also applies to any negative thoughts — regarding any subject whatever — because these negative impulses go out into the ether and attract other similar impulses, which regenerate and reinforce one another as sympathetic vibrations — like in the old-time regenerative radio receiver — and then come home to roost, many times more powerful and potent. Thoughts are things, not just vague wisps of nothingness. They are the most important part of you, because all actions start with thought, and thought influences all actions, past, present and even future. Our thoughts in previous incarnations influence our thinking today, and what we are thinking today will influence our thoughts in future incarnations. Viewed from a detached perspective, it all becomes one great trend of thought, and we are all parts of the whole, striving to uplift ourselves, whether we realize it or not, to eventual oneness with God. We have a long way to go, so now is a good time to start.

Think of everything as being good. If your environment does not suit you, remember it is of your own making, and only you are responsible for it. You can and should change it, until everything is according to your liking. This may take some time, of course, but this should be your goal. Things which you cannot change, you should accept for the present with good grace, and try to live comfortably with them. It is not the facts of your environment so much as how you perceive them that is most important. In other words, your thoughts about your environment are more important than is the actual environment itself. Put two people in the same environment, and one will be perfectly happy and contented, while the other will not. Is it the fault of the environment, or of the person?

You may have to reprogram your thoughts, repeating them time after time to your subconscious, so that the old negative thoughts will eventually be erased, and the new ones will take their place. It is well worth the effort.

Chapter Sixteen
Achieving Happiness

I have often thought it would be interesting to trace my ancestry back a few generations, and to see if I might be related to President James A. Garfield. I knew very little of his life, except that he was very poor, and that he served the shortest term of any of our presidents. Someone recently loaned me a very complete biography of Garfield, an old book containing almost 500 pages. I am glad I read it, because it tells of a man so remarkable, so outstanding, with such a brilliant mind and so many wonderful qualities, that reading about him was an inspiration. The reason I mention it here is to show how a person's attitude toward life is so important in guiding him into selecting the right alternatives for Egoic progress.

Throughout his life Garfield steadfastly refused to compromise with his high principles, yet he always found a way to come out on top. His father died when he was only 18 months old. The family of mother and four children lived in a crude log cabin in Ohio, with no income other than the food they could raise on their small farm. Jimmy's 11-year-old brother Thomas ran the farm. They suffered many and continuous hardships because of their extreme poverty, but through it all, Jimmy was a cheerful, happy boy, alert and anxious to learn at every opportunity. He began school at the age of three, having to be carried on the back of his older sister the three miles to school. At 10 years of age he was doing a man's work splitting wood and helping run the farm. He became a teacher at 16, successfully handling a class of unruly students who had run off every previous teacher, by winning them over with his charm and persuasion. This was where he first learned to overcome panic at standing up to a crowd or audience, and he later became one of the greatest public speakers of his day.

Garfield's life paralleled that of Abraham Lincoln in many ways, but Garfield was more of a scholar, well-read in almost every subject. He taught himself foreign languages, and was a diligent student of the Bible. He also taught himself enough law to be admitted to the bar in Ohio. His rise to the rank of major general in only two years during the Civil War, his election to Congress and finally his nomination and election to the presidency are all true stories that would be unbelievable if written as fiction. When Garfield was a child and some seemingly impossible task came up, his expression always was, "I can do it." And this positive approach to problems was his attitude throughout his life. But he did not go into situations blindly, trusting to luck. He prepared for them thoroughly and meticulously, always sure of himself, and this made his achievements seem almost too easy.

Garfield was assassinated after only three months in office, by a demented, disappointed office-seeker. His long struggle for life from July to September united the American people as nothing had been able to do previously. Prayers were said for him all over the world, and this may have been what sustained his breath of life for so long, with a bullet lying right behind his heart. His funeral was one of the most elaborate ever given as a tribute to a great man, loved by everyone. And yet, nowadays he is almost as forgotten as yesterday's newspaper. But there are lessons to be learned from his life, if we will only heed them. Garfield said he derived the most happiness from helping others — such as a student in Hiram College where Garfield was a professor, whose parents did not want him to continue his schooling. In such a case, Garfield went to the parents and tried to persuade them to change their minds by showing them the great advantages, financially as well as culturally, of more schooling.

Scientists are finding that everything has intelligence, from the simplest one-cell animals and plants to the more complex ones. How does a plant bend toward the light? How does plant osmosis occur? How do blood corpuscles squeeze through capillaries smaller in diameter than they are? Questions like these could be endless. A brain does not seem to be necessary for a cell or organism to function intelligently. In fact, there is intelligence in every atom and particle in the universe. A scientist noticed recently while examining some bacteria under a microscope that they all seemed to be headed in the same direction. Turning the slide around, he found them also reversing direction. To test his theory that they were influenced by the magnetic field of the earth, he traveled to the southern hemisphere, found some more bacteria of the same type, and examined them. Sure enough, they were all headed in a southerly direction, while the bacteria seen in the northern hemisphere were all traveling in a northerly direction. The solution to the puzzle was that tiny bits of iron in the one-cell bacteria line themselves up in a straight line, and this string of molecules acts as a compass needle after being magnetized by the earth's magnetic field. Nature made them this way so that they could always find their way into the soil, since the earth's magnetic field also points the compass needle downward as well as northward, or southward in the southern hemisphere. Birds and other animals are probably also sensitive to this effect.

We might say that these cells, and the smaller animals, are happy doing their thing, but we know that the higher animals are happy to perform tricks they know. Almost all animals can be taught to perform, and they love it. Bears ride bicycles, seals balance things on their noses, and so on.

Similarly, the human animal is usually happiest doing his thing, whatever it may be. Mind is the determining factor in happiness, not necessarily the physical conditions under which one lives. What you think you are is what you are. To become happier, elevate the quality of your thoughts. If your environment doesn't suit you, change it, by using your thought power, which is the strongest power there is. Learn to live in harmony with things which you cannot change immediately.

Since all things are electrical when reduced to their atomic or molecular components, and since thought is also electrical in nature, we can see that we are a part of the whole, not separate but a great oneness with God. Our minds cannot conceive of what is in store for us on the astral plane, because the mind is not designed to do that. But by proper living and elevating the level of our thoughts, it is possible to "re-wire" our brain so that we can become aware of at least some part of the astral plane. This ability will come to us when we are mentally and spiritually ready for it, not before, and without conscious effort on our part. Everyone has this latent gift, and it only needs to be developed. Everything in the universe is ordered — nothing happens by chance. As Albert Einstein said, "God does not play dice with the universe."

Let us now go over the main points of what we have covered. We have seen that our existence here, as well as the whole universe, is governed by Universal Law, which is all-encompassing. We learned that we have a definite purpose in life, which is the uplift of our consciousness and of mankind; and secondly, to help others in achieving a similar goal. We have seen how our universe originated, how it is constructed, and our place in it. And we have seen that our old concepts of matter and energy, time and space, and consciousness are not all correct, or only partially so. We know that matter, when scaled down in size, is not what it appears to us to be, but is actually an electromagnetic thought-form precipitated from the ether by consciousness. We learned that all matter was originally precipatated, and at some time will be dissolved in the same way. We know that the building blocks of this precipitation come from the ether, an all-pervading quiescent energy form that is always there, ready for an impulse from Mind to set it into action.

We have learned that the Ego or entity of the human consciousness is essentially Mind; the physical body is only a temporary vehicle. And we know that there are seven planes of existence, and that we are presently on the lowest of these, the one with the lowest vibrational or nutational level, the physical plane. We are all striving for advancement, whether we realize it or not, to ever-higher goals. We found that we have four bodies, all occupying the same space, without interference with one another.

We have read about The Brotherhoods and Their great work in guiding civilization and mankind to its present level of development. We have learned a little of Their philosophy, how it originated, how it was tested and proved through thousands of years and several civilizations. One thing especially important about The Brotherhoods' philosophy is The Twelve Great Virtues, which are among the qualities of character required for admission as an Initiate into The Brotherhoods, and which should be practiced by everyone who aspires to Egoic advancement in his daily life. The Great Virtues are: tolerance, patience, kindliness, forbearance, humility, sincerity, devotion, charity, courage, precision, efficiency, and discrimination.

We also briefly discussed karma and its effect on our lives, and the Black Mentalists (no reference to skin color), so named because they were masters of the art of black magic, which was practiced in ancient times. We read about their negative influence on civilization, even up to the present time.

We also noted that we are not prisoners of our environment; on the contrary, we create the environment we want simply by channeling our thoughts, desires and actions in that direction. We are now aware of the great power of thought, and of its nature, and of the absolute necessity of eliminating negativity from our thoughts in order to lead positively-oriented lives. The power of thought to influence events and our environment is far greater than we can even imagine; and the greater our faith and belief in its power, the greater it becomes.

In the next chapter will appear some excerpts from a book written over a hundred years ago by Henry Drummond, called *The Greatest Thing in the World*. Its suggestions for achieving happiness are as valid today as ever.

Chapter Seventeen
What Is Love?

To answer this great question, I have called on Henry Drummond and his book, *The Greatest Thing in the World*. This book has survived for a century of numerous publishers and editions, and can still be found on the shelves of bookstores. It is a religious book, but what I would call true religion — the simple doctrine of Christ's "Love one another."

"There is nothing capricious about religion. We do not get the soul in different ways, under different laws, from which we get the body and the mind. If a man does not exercise his arms, he develops no biceps; and if a man does not exercise his soul, he acquires no muscle in his soul, no strength of character, no vigor of moral fiber, nor beauty of spiritual growth. Love is not a thing of enthusiastic emotion, it is a rich, strong, manly, vigorous expression of the whole round christian character — the Christlike nature in its fullest development. And the constituents of this great character are only to be built up by ceaseless practice.

"What was Christ doing in the carpenter shop? Practicing. Though perfect, we read that He learned obedience, and grew in wisdom and in favor with God. Do not quarrel, therefore, with your lot in life. Do not complain of its never-ceasing cares, its petty environment, the vexations you have to stand, the small and sordid souls you have to live and work with. Above all, do not resent temptation; do not be perplexed because it seems to thicken around you more and more, and ceases not for agony nor prayer. That is your practice. That is the practice to which God appoints you; and it is having its work in making you patient, and humble, and generous and unselfish, and kind, and courteous.

"Do not judge the hand that is molding the still too shapeless image within you. It is growing more beautiful, though you see it not, and every touch of temptation may add to its perfection. Therefore, keep in the midst of life. Do not isolate yourself. Be among men, and among things, and among troubles, and among difficulties and obstacles. You remember Goethe's words: 'Talent develops itself in solitude, character in the stream of life.' Talent develops itself in solitude — the talent of prayer, of faith, of meditation, seeking the unseen; character grows in the stream of the world's life. That, chiefly, is where men are to learn Love. How? Now, how? Love itself can never be defined. Light is a something more than the sum of all its ingredients — a glowing, dazzling, tremulous ether. And Love is something more than all its elements — a palpitating, quivering, sensitive living thing. By synthesis of all the colors, men can make whiteness, they cannot make light. By synthesis of all the virtues, men can make virtue; they cannot make Love. How, then are we to have this transcendent living whole conveyed into our souls? We brace our wills to secure it. We lay down rules about it. We watch. We pray. But these things alone will not bring Love into our nature. Love is an *effect*. And only as we fulfill the right condition, can we have the effect produced. Contemplate the love of Christ, and you will love. Stand before the mirror, reflect Christ's character, and you will be changed into the same image of tenderness. There is no other way. You cannot love to order. You can only look at the lovely object, and fall in love with and grow to likeness to it. And so look at this perfect character, this perfect life, and upon the Cross of Calvary; and you must love Him. And loving Him, you must become like Him. Love begets love. It is a process of induction. Put a piece of iron in the presence of an electrified body, and that piece of iron becomes electrified. It is changed into a temporary magnet as long as it is in the presence of a permanent magnet, and as long as you leave the two side by side, they are both magnets alike.

"Remain side by side with Him who loves us, and gave Himself for us, and you too will become a permanent magnet, a permanent attractive force. And like Him, you will draw all men unto you. Like Him, you will be drawn unto all men. That is the inevitable effect of love. Any man who fulfills that cause must have that effect produced in him. Try to give up the idea that religion comes to us by chance, or by mystery, or by caprice. It comes to us by natural law, or by supernatural law, for all law is Divine.

"And that is how the love of God melts down the unlovely heart of man, and begets in him the new creature who is patient and gentle and humble and unselfish. And there is no other way to get it. There is no mystery about it. We love others, we love everybody, we love our enemies, because He first loved us.

"Can you tell me anything that is going to last? In speaking of this, there were many things Paul did not condescend to name. He did not mention money, fortune or fame; but he picked out the great things of his time, the things the best men thought had something in them, and brushed them peremptorily aside. Paul had no charge against these things in themselves. All he said about them was that they would not last. They were great things, but not supreme things. There were things beyond them. What we are stretches past what we do, what we possess. Many things that men denounce as sins are not sins; but they are temporary. And that is a favorite argument of the New Testament. John says of the world, not that it is wrong, but that it 'passeth away.' There is a great deal in the world that is delightful and beautiful; there is a great deal in it that is great and engrossing; but it will not last. All that is in the world, the lust of the eye, the lust of the flesh, and the pride of life, are but for a little while. Love not the world therefore; nothing that it contains is worth the life and consecration of an immortal soul. The immortal soul must give itself to something that is immortal. And the only immortal things are these: 'Now abideth faith, hope, love, but the greatest of these is love.'

"To love abundantly is to live abundantly; and to love forever is to live forever. Hence eternal life is inextricably bound up with love. We want to live forever for the same reason that we want to live tomorrow. Why do you want to live tomorrow? It is because there is someone who loves you, and whom you want to see tomorrow and be with, and love back. There is no other reason that we should want to live on than that we are loved and beloved. It is when a man has no one to love him that he commits suicide. So long as he has friends, those who love him and whom he loves, he will live, because to live is to love. Be it but the love of a dog, it will keep him in life, but let that go and he has no contact with life, no reason to live. He dies by his own hand. Eternal life is also to know God, and God is Love. This is Christ's own definition. Ponder it. 'This is life eternal, that they might know Thee, the only true God, and Jesus Christ, whom Thou has sent.'

"Love must be eternal. It is what God is. On the last analysis, then, love is life, love never faileth, and life never faileth, so long as there is love. That is the philosophy of what Paul is showing us; the reason why, in the nature of things, Love should be the supreme thing — because it is going to last, because in the nature of things it is an Eternal Life. It is a thing that we are living now, not that we get when we die; that we shall have a poor chance of getting when we die, unless we are living now. No worse fate can befall a man than to live and grow old unloving and unloved. To be lost is to live in an unregenerate condition, loveless and unloved; and to be saved is to love; and he that dwelleth in love dwelleth already in God. For God is Love.

"In the Book of Matthew, where the Judgment Day is depicted for us, in the imagery of One seated on a throne and dividing the sheep from the goats, the test of a man then is not 'How have I believed?' but 'How have I loved?' The test of religion, the final test of religion, is not religiousness, but love. I say the final test of religion at that great Day is not religiousness, but Love, not what I have believed, not what I have done, not what I have achieved, but how I have discharged the common charities of life. Sins of commission in that awful indictment are not even referred to.

"By what we have not done, *by sins of omission,* we are judged. It could not be otherwise, for the withholding of love is the negation of the spirit of Christ, the proof that we never knew Him, that for us He lived in vain. The words which all of us shall one Day hear sound not of theology but of life, not of churches and saints but of the hungry and the poor, not of creeds and doctrines but of shelter and clothing, not of Bibles and prayer books but of cups of cool water in the name of Christ."

Chapter Eighteen
The Lower Centers of Consciousness

At this point we have become acquainted with the Philosophy of The Brotherhoods, in particular the Twelve Great Virtues, and we have investigated the nature of love. Now I would like to present a condensed version of the book, *Handbook to Higher Consciousness,* by Ken Keyes, Jr., published by Ken Keyes Center, 790 Commercial Avenue, Coos Bay, Oregon 97420. The complete book is readily available at bookstores, if you wish to explore more deeply the material that follows. This is a modernized and westernized version of the teachings of the religions of the far east, and it should help you to make faster progress in your quest for higher consciousness and therefore greater happiness.

In the early days of man's existence on Earth, his mind became programmed, through necessity, for instant reaction to the threat of attack by wild beasts or enemies, so that he adopted an attitude of "fight or flight" to all unfriendly advances by man or beast. Although man no longer needs this type of programming, it is still with us to some degree, and must be eliminated from our consciousness before we can adopt the principles necessary for Egoic advancement. Among the points we have just read about to develop a higher level of consciousness, one was to love yourself and another was to love others. Mr. Keyes expresses it as "love everyone unconditionally — including yourself." That word "unconditionally" is the big hurdle for most of us. Yet that is the way Christ teaches us, and that is the way we all must go if we expect to advance spiritually. The teachings of Buddha have also played an important part in the philosophy of Mr. Keyes' book, as well as many others, who are acknowledged in the book. In fact, the philosophies of East and West are gradually being broadened and drifting closer together, as man learns more about himself and the universe.

Almost all the activities of our minds, such as reasoning, emotions, feelings, sensations and talking, fall into one of three categories, namely security, sensation or power. If you check on your thoughts for a while, you will see that this is true. Some of our thoughts fall into the class of addictions to a pre-programmed habit of thinking, in one of the categories mentioned above. These so-called addictions are like a drug — our subconscious tells our conscious mind that we need this thing or idea, and must have it, and the longer we give in to it the stronger the influence of the subconscious becomes. We could be referring to any activity of the mind, such as a desire for food, or for a certain kind of food, or a belief that this or that physical disorder is inevitable, such as a common cold or aging, or endless other thoughts that are so ingrained into our consciousness that we accept them as facts or convictions.

In all of our thinking on the three lower centers of activity, these addictions play hob with the reasoning power of our minds and with our emotions and feelings, and in order to eliminate these addictions we must reprogram our minds. These addictions expend a large amount of our energy, too, and after our minds have been reprogrammed we free ourselves of this drain on our system, and we can then make use of this energy on a higher consciousness level. To do this, we change our addictions into preferences. Now we do not need to stew and fret if we do not get our way in some matter, but accept the facts as they develop

The Lower Centers of Consciousness 127

and keep our "cool," because it was only a preference anyway, not an addiction. This saves nervous energy so we can use it to reason our way out of the dilemma. When your subconscious learns definitely that you are in control, it will help you in every way, even while you sleep. Either you control it, or it controls you, by default.

Over 99 percent of the people living in the Western World live on lower consciousness levels characterized by trying to find enough of such things as security, sex, prestige, sensory stimulus, money, power and status, or collection of objects. This endless struggle yields lives of resentment, worry, suspicion, anger, jealousy, shyness and fear. Everything people tell themselves they must have in order to be happy ends up yielding more frustration than joy. The more successful a person is in making money, collecting skills and possessions, and acquiring wealth and position, the less loving, peaceful and contented he may find himself. And yet it is not these things in and of themselves that create an unhappy life — it is the internal mental addiction or desire for them that, minute by minute, keeps one from enjoying life. Addictions (or emotion-backed demands) bring fear of non-fulfillment; jealousy that someone may steal our source of fulfillment; anger when someone thwarts us; cynicism if constantly undersupplied; paranoia if constantly threatened; boredom if we are making no progress toward satisfying our addictions; anxiety if we are worried about being worried; and unhappiness when the outside world does not supply us with whatever we are addicted to. Since the nature of life is such that we win some and lose some, an addicted person has no chance of living a happy, loving, peaceful, wise and effective life. And the addictive programming is not necessary to find and enjoy that which we prefer in life.

You are ready for growth into the happiness of higher consciousness when you realize the utter futility of trying to live a beautiful life by your efforts to rearrange or change the world of people and things outside of you to fit your addictions and desires. You will find you have only to rearrange your own personal, automatically programmed responses to life situations, most of which are childhood hangups.

As you work toward higher levels of consciousness, you will find that you have always had enough to be happy. It is the patterns in your head that make you unhappy, although you usually blame the people and conditions outside you for your unhappiness. Your journey into higher consciousness can enable you to be loving, peaceful, wise, and free of a constant barrage of unpleasant emotional feelings.

Mr. Keyes' living love concept offers you four advantages in your adventure into higher consciousness:

1.) For many people it can be one of the most powerful and rapid ways for growth into higher consciousness that has ever been available to mankind.

2.) It does not require you to detach yourself from your present.

3.) Once you thoroughly understand the system, it is not essential to have a teacher to continue your growth. Your life will be your best teacher, for you will discover that you are always putting yourself into learning situations that are ideal for your growth. The programming that you most need to change has an unerring way of putting you into situations that can make you aware of the exact inner work you should be doing.

4.) When you use the living love way to find the love, inner peace, wisdom and effectiveness of higher consciousness, your inner work on yourself immediately adds to your enjoyment of life. Happiness becomes not a distant goal, but an ever-growing part of your here-and-now.

Almost every way we have been taught to work toward happiness only reinforces the feelings and activities that make us unhappy. This is an important point that must be understood. The way we were taught to be happy can't possibly work. Unless we see this clearly, we cannot progress to higher consciousness. Here is why:

Most of us assume that our desires (backed up by emotional feelings) are the true guides to doing the things that will make us happy. But no one has yet found happiness by using emotion-backed desires as guides. Flashes of pleasure, yes; happiness, no. Our wants and desires are so seductive, they masquerade as "needs" that must be satisfied so that we can be happy at last. Finding just the right person to love, whom our addiction tells us will make us happy, results in temporary pleasure, but not lasting love. As we grow in our path to higher consciousness, we find that it is more important to be the right person than to find the right person.

We must deeply understand why all of our negative emotions are misleading guides to effective action in life situations. Our negative emotions are simply the result of an extensive pattern of scars and wounds that we have experienced. And these wounds make us perceive differences that cause us to be uptight, instead of perceiving similarities that enable us to understand and love. The present programming of our emotions makes us see other people and the conditions of the world around us as threats, potentially dangerous to our well-being. We then respond with adrenalin, faster heartbeat, increased blood sugar, and other jungle survival responses that prepare us for fight or flight. We are trapped in our ways of perceiving the world around us.

But no one, nor any situation, need be felt as an emotional threat or danger when we see things with the clearer perception of higher consciousness. All problems either have solutions or they don't. Either you can do something about them — here and now — or you can't. If you can do something about them here and now, do it, even if it is only a first step. It saps your energy to be worried or anxious about a problem. Do what you can do, but don't be addicted to the results, or you will add more worry for yourself. If you can't do anything about it here and now, don't sap your energy worrying about it. Worry and anxiety are absolutely unnecessary, and only add to the difficulty in taking effective action. You must absolutely convince yourself of the lack of utility of these negative emotions, or you will be retarded in your growth to higher consciousness. For only an emotionally calm biocomputer (or mind) can see clearly and wisely and come up with effective solutions to problems.

Chapter Nineteen
The Love Center of Consciousness

The Law of Higher Consciousness is :

Love Everyone Unconditionally — Including Yourself.

We have never been taught how to love unconditionally. Almost all of our loving has been motivated by desires programmed into us at an early age. Most of our love experiences have taught us that we must earn and deserve love before we can have it — and that others must deserve our love. This is conditional love. It is like a barter or a business transaction. It is no wonder that our well-meaning but unskilled attempts to love usually end in separation and alienation. Real love is simply accepting another person, completely and unconditionally. We realize that no matter how intensely we strive for worldly attainments, we all seek love and oneness on the consciousness level. We are all on the journey to higher consciousness. Some of us are hearing the messages life has to offer us and are working consciously to eliminate our addictions. Others are not progressing so rapidly because they do not yet know consciously how to work on themselves.

We must also learn to love ourselves — right here and now. We need to feel that no matter how horribly we have judged our past actions, each day our life begins anew. We are all children as long as we are programmed with our lower class addictions. So we must accept the melodramas we get involved in as we live out our current crop of addictions. This too is a part of life and growth. The key to throwing off your addictions is instant emotional acceptance of the here and now — the emotional acceptance of the previously unacceptable. When our emotions are triggered, we cannot perceive clearly our actual life situation. Our biocomputer then sends a flow of information to our consciousness in which sensation and alienation are emphasized. We create a badly warped evaluation of the situation based on our addictive programming. When this happens, we magnify differences and suppress similarities between ourselves and others, and this destroys our ability to love unconditionally.

Mr. Keyes' book lists twelve pathways to higher consciousness, which are given below. These are the cornerstones on which his Living Love theme is based, and they are divided into four groups, as follows:

FREEING MYSELF

1.) I am freeing myself from security, sensation and power addictions that make me try to forcefully control situations in my life, and thus destroy my serenity and keep me from loving myself and others.

By reprogramming our addictions into preferences, we free ourselves from the limitations of addictions by eliminating the lower-class reactions triggered by our brain in the past. We do not need to change our activities to do this; we can still prefer a certain thing, but it is no longer necessary for our happiness.

2.) I am discovering how my addictions create false illusions of the changing world around me.

We see things not as they are, but as we are. Every addiction distorts our effective processing, on both conscious and unconscious levels, of the enormous flood of information that is continually flowing in through our five senses to our biocomputer. The reticular network system of our brain screens the data it sends to the central cerebral center, the master analyzer. This network can close down your consciousness and put you to sleep, or turn up your consciousness and awaken you. This neutral structure performs the function that is often referred to as the ego; not the same as the Ego referred to previously describing the Mind or Soul of man. The reticular activity network selects from the information received by it, which of the information is to go into our consciousness. It does this by following the information that has been put into it since infancy. Thus, your programmed addictions determine your experience of the world. In this way, you gradually build up an illusory version of the people and things in the world. For the mind is such that whatever it believes is true is continually reinforced by feedback that molds our perception. One should always be aware that his head creates his world. Your addiction patterns — your expectations, desires, attachments, demands, mental models — dominate your perception of the world around you. It is only when you become free of your addictive programming that you can perceive how things really interact in your world.

3.) I welcome the opportunity (even if painful) that my minute-to-minute experience offers me, to become aware of the addictions I must reprogram to be liberated from my robot-like emotional patterns.

To help in identifying your addictions, watch for emotions that make you feel uncomfortable. If you have removed all your addictions, you should feel comfortable all of the time. As these addictions come up, change them to preferences, or eliminate them entirely. Your moment-to-moment becomes interesting and real when you experience everything as a step in your growth toward higher consciousness. Thus, you are turning negative thoughts into positive ones, and will be well on your way to happiness.

BEING HERE NOW

4.) I always remember that I have everything I need in order to enjoy the here and now — unless I am letting my consciousness be dominated by demands and expectations based on the dead past or the imagined future.

Realize the importance to you of living your life moment-by-moment, and enjoying the here and now to its fullest. *The past is gone, the future is not yet here, and you have everything you need to enjoy life at this moment.* When something intrudes into your life, do not let it trigger your addictive emotions, but let it be just another lesson in teaching you advancement toward higher consciousness. Enjoy what you do have, rather than worrying about what you don't have.

5.) I take full responsibility here and now for everything I experience, for it is my own programming that creates my actions, and also influences the reactions of people around me.

It is easy to lay the blame on someone else for conditions that do not agree with our addictions. This is an evasion. When you realize that you create your own environment, and you alone are responsible for it, you can free yourself from this feeling of frustration, anger or whatever addiction it may be, and turn the feeling into one of opposite polarity — joy and happiness. Your feelings, attitudes and actions produce similar reactions in others around you. These reactions, in turn, affect your reactions to them, so an atmosphere is created that reflects the attitudes of all concerned.

6.) I accept myself completely here and now, and consciously experience everything I feel, think, say and do, including my emotion-backed addictions, as a necessary part of my growth into higher consciousness.

This point is based on the instant emotional acceptance of that which you previously found unacceptable in your life. Acceptance simply means you won't cause yourself emotional conflict because of your current perceptions. It does not mean that you are not free to do as you prefer to do. In order to consciously observe yourself and your addictions, think of your world as a stage and you as one of the audience, observing the drama of life from a detached viewpoint.

INTERACTION WITH OTHERS

7.) I open myself genuinely to all people by being willing to communicate my deepest feelings, since hiding in any degree keeps me stuck in my illusion of separateness from other people.

As you begin to uplevel all your addictions to the status of preferences, or eliminate them altogether, you will discover that you no longer have anything to hide from other people, and it then feels good to communicate with others exactly what you are experiencing. In communicating with others, we break down the wall of isolation that is built up around us when we hide our true feelings.

8.) I feel with loving compassion the problems of others, without getting caught up emotionally in their predicaments that are offering them messages they need for their growth.

Compassion means that you realize the problems and suffering of others because of playing out their addictions of security, sensation or power, but that you also realize that they must learn themselves from their experiences in order to free themselves and grow into higher consciousness. When you can help someone with a feeling of love and oneness — you just do it, because it feels good to you. When you feel oneness with another, there is no giver or receiver — there is just us here. It is like one hand washing another. You just let energy flow through you. As you free yourself of your addictions you will liberate a continuous stream of energy, which will flow into loving and serving people around you.

9.) I act freely when I am tuned in, centered and loving, but if possible I avoid acting when I am emotionally upset and depriving myself of the wisdom that flows from love and expanded consciousness.

When you are emotionally upset, you energize the addictive patterns of others as well as yourself. It is difficult to reach an understanding under these conditions, and destroys the peace and serenity that comes with calm communication. There is some conflict between this pathway and number seven, but always remember that you cannot hide your emotions or feelings for long if you wish to be conscious, perceptive and loving.

DISCOVERING MY CONSCIOUS-AWARENESS

10.) I am continually calming the restless scanning of my rational mind, in order to perceive the finer energies that enable me to unitively merge with everything around me.

The activity of the rational mind is generally sparked by the lower-consciousness addictions of security, sensation or power. This is the restless scanning referred to above, and it limits our ability to control our thoughts and to think calmly and effectively. When the addictions are reduced to preferences, our minds are freed from random compulsive thoughts, and can function according to our direction, so that we are constantly in touch with that deep, calm place inside of us from which we peacefully, lovingly and blissfully watch the dramas of our lives.

11.) I am constantly aware of which of the seven centers of consciousness I am using, and feel my energy, perceptiveness, love and inner peace growing as I open all of the centers of consciousness.

The Seven Centers of Consciousness, which are explained later, consist of a seven-step scale that can tell you each moment of your life exactly where you are in your journey toward higher consciousness. When you have risen above the lower three centers of security, sensation and power, you are on your way to the fourth or love center, where you learn to love everyone unconditionally. The next three are called the cornucopia center, the conscious-awareness center and the cosmic-consciousness center.

12.) I am perceiving everyone, including myself, as an awakening being who is here to claim his birthright to the higher consciousness planes of unconditional love and oneness.

Everyone has the capacity for clear perception, wisdom, effectiveness, peace and love, but unless one works consciously toward higher consciousness, this hidden splendor within may be smothered by the addictive games that keep one isolated. It will help if we regard ourselves and others as fellow travelers on the journey to awakening. When you are in doubt as to whether or not to do something, ask yourself whether it will make you feel more separate or more loving to others in your world.

Chapter Twenty
Extending the Love Center

The three lower centers of consciousness cannot bring you enough security, sensation or power to make you happy continuously, because they cause constant distortion in perceiving people and situations. These centers keep you from loving unconditionally, and make you view people as objects instead of as being just like you. Those lower centers subject you to multiple emotional strains, forcing the brain to choose between them, and dulling its ability to perceive clearly. Have an awareness of where you are, from moment to moment, from your detached vantage point of the Living Love way. And each time you use one of these methods you will find that you are becoming more peaceful and loving in a situation that previously would have resulted in your emotionally thrashing around and upsetting yourself and others.

A thumbnail description of the Seven Centers of Consciousness will be given here:

1.) The security center. This addiction makes one preoccupied with getting enough food, shelter or whatever one equates with security. One's consciousness is thus dominated by a continual struggle to get enough to feel secure.

2.) The sensation center. Victims of this addiction are dominated by the search for new or more sensations of such things as sex, food, music, entertainment or a thousand other things.

3.) The power center. This concerns the domination of people and situations, and increasing your pride and prestige, as well as countless other forms of hierarchy, manipulation and control.

4.) The love center. At this center you are transcending subject-object relationships and are learning to see the world with the feelings and harmonies of flowing acceptance. You see yourself in everyone, and everyone in yourself. You feel compassion for those caught in the dramas of security, sensation and power. You are beginning to love and accept everyone unconditionally, even yourself.

5.) The cornucopia center. When your consciousness is illuminated by this center, you experience the friendliness of the world you are creating. You begin to realize that you have always lived in a perfect world. To the degree that you still have addictions, the perfection lies in giving you the experience you need to get free of your emotion-backed demands. As you reprogram your addictions, the perfection will be experienced as a continuous enjoyment of the here and now in your life. As you become more loving and accepting, the world becomes a "horn of plenty" that gives you more than you need to be happy.

6.) The conscious-awareness center. It is liberating to have a center from which your conscious-awareness watches your body and mind perform on the five lower centers. This is a meta-center from which you nonjudgmentally witness the drama of your body and mind. From here you learn to impartially observe your social roles and life games from a position that is free from fear and vulnerability.

7.) The cosmic-consciousness center. When you live fully in the sixth center of consciousness, you are ready to transcend self-awareness and become true awareness. At this ultimate level you are one with everything — you are love, peace, energy, beauty, wisdom, clarity, effectiveness, and oneness.

Considering the lowest level of consciousness first, the security level, it is not the outside conditions of your life that make you feel secure or insecure, but the way you have programmed your mind to react to outside conditions. Your particular security addictions may be different from anyone else's, and as you get the things you need to make you feel secure, you may find that these things still do not satisfy your security needs. In fact, there is no such thing as absolute security, and life would be dull if there were no element of risk involved. The security center of consciousness is very demanding, and strongly pulls your consciousness away from the higher levels. Your security will increase as you replace your emotional fears with the calm reasoning of consciousness. To rid yourself of your security addiction, think back over your life and realize that your fears did not help you to meet the situations which you overcame, and that feelings of emotional insecurity are unnecessary to your here and now life, and to your future advancement. When you are governed by your security addictions, you isolate yourself because you are making others into subject-object relationships in order to manipulate them to meet your security needs, and for this reason you cannot love others unconditionally as you will be able to on the higher levels of consciousness.

The second center of consciousness, the sensation center, traps many people with their addictions of pleasurable sensation equating it with happiness. This can never be true, because sensation is a fleeting thing, requiring more and more sensation for its momentary fulfillment, and eventually leading to boredom and unhappiness. When sensation is enjoyed on a preference rather than on an addiction basis, from a higher consciousness level, then it can add to one's happiness as a part of the here and now of his life. The sensation level of consciousness takes less energy from a person than the security level, and does not tend to isolate him from others, but wisdom, peace and serenity are still not yet in sight.

The third or power center of consciousness is the last of the centers that can never provide you with "enough" to make you happy. Most of the people of the world are addicted to these three centers. When you live in the lower centers, you live in a competitive world, having a subject-object relationship with others, and engrossed in moves and counter-moves to win an advantage. Addictions here include money, prestige, status symbols, and any manipulation of others to satisfy your power needs. To the degree that your moment-to-moment consciousness is biased by security, sensation and power, you are trapped in the lower consciousness folkways of our culture — and you are not finding enough in life to be happy. You are ready for the next step toward higher consciousness when you deeply realize the utter futility of trying to make it in life, using these lower consciousness levels. This does not necessarily mean that you must drastically change your external activities. For what you renounce is your addictive demands, and not necessarily the things you are doing. You will grow in happiness when you realize that all of this emotion-backed addiction is not who you really are. It is just ego-backed programming that you picked up on your way to where you are now. Your energy will enormously increase, and your sleep needs decrease, as you give up guarding the various manifestations of your security, sensation and power addictions.

One of the bonuses of higher consciousness is that when you give it up, you get it all back. What you give up are your inner addictive demands — what you get back is more of everything you need to be happy. When you operate from the fourth center of consciousness, you will find that doors will open for you that never would be opened when you operated from the lower centers of consciousness.

We have seen that it is possible to achieve great success externally from the three lower centers of security, sensation and power, but it is not possible to achieve through them genuine peace, serenity and happiness. The fourth and fifth centers will start us on the journey to attaining these goals. Here you emotionally accept everyone and everything instantly, while still being entitled to your preferences. How do you love everyone unconditionally, no matter what they do or say? You can do this only by transcending your lower level addictions — for it is only your emotional programming that disturbs you when events outside you do not conform to your programmed demands. As your addictions melt away, you experience everyone and everything around you in a different way. You view them not in terms of how they meet your addictive needs — for you are losing those "needs" — but in terms of the reality of the here and now. You realize that everyone is creating a world in which he has to live out his addictions, as you yourself are doing. When you notice the hollowness and suffering these addictions cause, you achieve insights that help you get free from them.

As you learn to live more and more in the love center you will begin to find that you are creating a new world in which your consciousness resides. People and conditions are no longer a threat to you, for no one can threaten your preferences. "Others" can only threaten your addictions, and you are losing those fast. Soon your mind will create no "others."

When you are operating in the fourth level of consciousness you will tend to elevate others to that level also, because they will find that it is not necessary for them to be tense and competitive, and they will experience the same feelings that you are experiencing on the higher levels. Thus a seed is planted for their awakening. Also, when you are on the higher levels your relaxed blood vessels allow your circulatory system to operate more efficiently, and this will result in improved blood circulation, which benefits your whole body.

As you spend more time in the fourth center you will find that you enjoy touching people more and more. Now that you are seldom paranoid, you can enjoy the beautiful feelings of warmth and oneness that you can experience when you make contact not only through words, sight and sound, but also through your touch receptors. As you break through the illusion of duality and separation, you begin to realize that it was only your head that kept you from loving people unconditionally. It was not their actions, as you had been conditioned to believe.

In the fourth center of consciousness you experience "work" as an expression of love and caring. "Work" is no longer performed unconsciously or mechanically, with the feeling that one can fully enjoy life again when the job is done. You will increase your growth into higher consciousness by learning to flow energy into the needs of others as though they were your own needs. Selfless service is a beautiful way to get free of the three lower centers of consciousness.

The fifth center of consciousness, or cornucopia center, is an extension of the love center, and a natural development from it, in which you feel that the world is a friendly place, and that you feel at home in it. Instead of shying away from people and situations, you now feel that you have nothing to be afraid of. You will find friendships that you could never have found before. You will find yourself exploring areas of life that you would never have experienced previously because of your security, sensation and power addictions. You now experience them in an open, relaxed way, rather than in a preconceived, judgmental way. This openness is beginning to let you experience life in an almost miraculous way. Since you are open to most life situations which were problems to you, you now find beautiful solutions. Events are seen in terms of results and happenings instead of peoples' attitudes toward you. You will begin to experience your life as one miraculous happening after another. But this transformation could have happened at any time in your life, because you have created it, simply because of your increasing openness to people and things around you. You begin to see that the miracle was always there, but it took place in its own court — because you were too busy hassling yourself with your addictions and trying to manipulate people and things around you. Life is now offering you a cornucopia, or a horn of plenty.

And the miracle of cornucopia consciousness occurs because of three powerful factors that automatically aid you when you substantially reduce the number of addictions you are guarding.

1.) Since addictions waste your energy, you will now have a huge supply of energy to use as you prefer.

2.) Since addictions blind you, you will now have clear insight into what you should do or not do in various situations.

3.) Since addictions separate you from others, you will now live in a loving energy field, in which people love you and help you.

As you gain insight into the fifth center, you will begin to feel that you live in a friendly world that will always give you "enough." You will also begin to deeply feel that you live in a perfect world, from the standpoint of providing you with the experiences you need for your development as a conscious being. In this center you experience people and situations around you as part of a generous world that constantly offers you everything you need to be happy. Who could ask for anything more? And yet there is more, as you grow toward the last two centers of consciousness.

Chapter Twenty One
Aids to Attaining Your Goal

The sixth, or conscious-awareness center of consciousness is a calm, peaceful place deep inside you where you can watch the drama of your life from a detached viewpoint. You do not judge or evaluate in any way. You just witness yourself performing in all of the other five centers of consciousness. You will still want to play an active part in the world around you. You will still be learning various things, interacting with people, and doing your part in building a more beautiful world by living a conscious life. But *you* will not be doing it. It will be only your body and mind that are involved in these daily dramas of working, playing, feeling, doing, etc. Your conscious-awareness will be watching it all from a peaceful place deep inside you. Even if your body and mind go through the manifestations of anger or jealousy, you are aware that you are only playing out one of your addictive roles in your dramatic repertory. For you are just silently watching your body and mind picking up the cues and saying your lines as others recite their lines in the daily drama of life.

Each of us creates a world that is generated by the centers of consciousness that we are using in today's script of the cosmic play. The other actors are there for the purpose of helping you in your consciousness growth. But your higher consciousness is out in the "audience" watching your body and mind interacting with other bodies and minds on stage. And you do everything you do and say as part of your growth toward freedom from your addictive traps.

The world is here for us to enjoy, but we can totally enjoy it only when we are free from identifying with the roles we play in the drama of life. We need a way to discriminate between what we essentially are, and the motivational models that generate our behavior.

To get free of our identification with the social games in which we are now trapped, we must clearly see the games for what they are. It can be helpful to experience a book such as Ruth Benedict's *Pattern of Culture*.

We gradually learn that we are not the personalities that our egos are defending so valiantly. If we are not our personalities, this collection of motivations that we have picked up from our society, just what, or who, are we? Many of us identify ourselves with our bodies — this structure of bone and muscle. When our body is transmitting a sensation of pain to our brain, our ego tends to focus our attention on the pain, so we identify completely with the pain. As we grow into higher consciousness, we increasingly realize that we are not the bodies we live in. Our bodies are just the homes of our consciousness. The real you is the awareness of your consciousness. Think of the events, thoughts and feelings going through your head as being projected onto a television screen inside your head, and your conscious-awareness as the watcher of the screen. The events on the screen may show pain and suffering, or beauty and pleasure, but you as the watcher are pure awareness, just watching the events go by on the screen of your life.

The essential you is perfect, has always been perfect, and will always be perfect. There is nothing you can do to alter the essential you. And this perfection does not need to be guarded with ego. When you realize who and what you really are, your ego can relax, and you can really enjoy your life. For nothing poses either threat or "absolute necessity" for you any longer. You can truly enjoy being the essential

Aids to Attaining Your Goal

you — and only then can you totally and continuously enjoy the unfolding drama that your life brings you. As you learn to identify the essential you with your conscious-awareness, instead of with the social and individual "stuff" that your ego has backed up in the past, you deeply and continuously enjoy both the drama of your life, and the perfect being that you naturally are.

The seventh center of consiousness is called the cosmic-consciousness center. You will observe that your growth toward the higher centers may fall naturally into three phases:

1.) As your consciousness begins to dwell more and more in the love center and cornucopia center, you will begin to develop a multi-centered perception that will enable you to see all of your thoughts and actions from each of the first five centers.

2.) Continuing the multi-centered awareness, you learn to witness yourself on the detached conscious-awareness center, of higher consciousness. It is all the same from the conscious-awareness center.

3.) You go behind the conscious-awareness center to the selfless, unitive space of the cosmic-consciousness center. In the sixth center there is still some duality. There is still a fine line of separation between you and the world. On the seventh level of consciousness, one is catapulted from self-awareness into pure awareness. In other words, one is no longer witnessing oneself. The body, mind, senses and conscious-awareness are not separated. In this center one does not experience security, sensation, power, love and fulfillment — he *is* security, sensation, power, love and fulfillment. The highest state of consciousness is attained by reprogramming what is called the "self." One's thought activity is calmed. The direction of perception has shifted through a phase of loving acceptance to a unity with everything in the environment.

The seventh center is extremely difficult to attain. Of all the people in the world, there may be only a hundred who live consistently in that center. Achieving it usually requires a detached life style and a long period of consciousness growth practice. Even preferences must be eliminated to reach this growth center.

When you have eliminated about 99 percent of your addictions, the amount remaining will probably be very subtle, and will not interfere with happiness. The love and cornucopia centers are totally adequate to enable you to live a happy, fulfilled, wise, effective and enjoyable life. It is worth while knowing about the two highest centers, but do not let them become addictions.

There are five ways in which you can work on yourself to accomplish your goal to higher consciousness.

The first is:

Memorize the twelve pathways, and use them to guide you through your life situations. The twelve pathways will show you what it means to be truly alive. You will look back to your present state of consciousness and realize that you have been far more dead than alive. Everything you need will come to you in a seemingly miraculous fashion as you live with these pathways. The peace, love and effectiveness that you have always wanted will be yours.

The second way is:

Be aware at all times of which center of consciousness you are experiencing. Your awareness of which center you are using, and your use of the twelve pathways to continually guide you, are the living love ways to meditate. And you do this all the time during your busy life, so that your entire life becomes meditation. In this way, meditation is not a holy ritual, to be performed once or twice a day. It is a method for consistently seeing things clearly and consciously — here and now.

The third way:

Become more consciously conscious of the cause-effect relationship between your addictions and the resulting unhappiness.

To use the third method effectively, it is essential that you become increasingly conscious of each of your addictions, because you can't eliminate them until you can identify them. Many addictions will rapidly melt away as soon as you consciously experience that the suffering they cause is actually due to the addiction. Some of the deeper addictions require more work to rid yourself of them. Consciously connect all of the suffering in your life with the addictive, emotion-backed models and expectations that you keep telling yourself you must have to be happy. Resolve now that you will never again try to convince yourself that others are the cause of your suffering — thus perpetuating your entrapment in the security, sensation and power programming. To break loose from these lower-consciousness traps, you must always take full responsibility for what you are experiencing, and get to work as quickly as possible on the addiction that causes you to reject emotionally what people are doing or saying. By taking full responsibility for your addictions, you get your rational mind and ego working for you to rid yourself of the addiction, instead of working against you, to help change yourself instead of changing the outside world.

When you reprogram, you use your will and determination to give clear firm instructions to your biocomputer. You tell it that you want it to function in a different way in processing incoming data in the future. This means that with intensity and conviction you put a new operating instruction into your mind. Reprogramming works most effectively if you repeat it many times.

Number four:
Use the catalyst *all ways us living love* for cognitive centering.

Your growth into higher consciousness can be more rapid if you keep a catalyst going in your mind as a foreground figure against which all of your sensations, feelings and thoughts are the background. This constant repetition helps you to calm your mind, to increase your powers of concentration, to broaden your powers of perception, to permit your intuitive wisdom to emerge, to free you from your addictions, and to keep you feeling great.

Method number five:
Consciousness focusing.

Consciousness focusing is based on the fact that your emotional programming is established by whatever you tell yourself with strong feelings whenever you are in pain or suffering. Actually, you have been using this principle all of your life.

When you are calm you have the best opportunity to reprogram your mind — but not your emotional addictions. When you are emotionally upset, you have a superlative opportunity to reprogram your addictions. Whatever you tell yourself at this time is absolutely crucial. So be sure to blame all of your uptightness on your addictive programming. Whatever you tell yourself when you are emotionally upset will play a prominent part in what you will have to live with in the future. In reprogramming your addictions, find the phrases and thoughts that generate the strongest emotions when you are upset. Shout, cry, pound on the table, stamp on the floor or whatever arouses your emotions. Reprogramming phrases should include new insights you have gained while examining the situation which is bothering you. These phrases and thoughts must be repeated over and over until your biocomputer has no doubt that this is what you want. Develop the confidence that you can absolutely be the master of yourself. Keep telling yourself that you programmed yourself many years ago, and that you can reprogram yourself as your knowledge and awareness increase. You are not the victim of circumstances or conditions — you did it all yourself, and you alone are responsible. What you think today determines your environment and emotional makeup tomorrow. When you have freed yourself from all your addictions, demands and expectations, which are the cause of your negative emotions and unhappiness, you can enjoy continuously the beauty and contentment of your life.

It should be noted that reprogramming your addictions is not repression. Repression means that you do not express your feelings because you are afraid of the consequences. Repression is one of the most harmful things you can do to yourself. What we are suggesting is that you take the energy generated by an emotion, and turn it into reprogramming the addiction into a preference. You thus do not repress the energy, but actually use it constructively, and avoid triggering the rational mind into feelings of negative polarity. As you gain control over your mind, you will be able to select the thoughts and emotions you desire, and reject those that are negative. A conscious being knows that life always works best when we operate from a loving plane that lets us experience other people, no matter what they do or say, as being no different from ourselves.

Our biocomputer works best when it is calm and undisturbed by irritations and emotions of anger, fear, anxiety and so on.

It is then able to tune in to the more subtle aspects of the people and situations around us. Our insight and perceptiveness increase a hundred-fold. You will find that your inherent wisdom guides you so that you can respond to whatever situation develops in your life. A traditional way of calming the rational mind is through meditation. If you sit quietly and concentrate on one object or condition, and try to put all random thoughts out of your mind, or if they persist, let them go through and then return to the concentration. You can gradually train your mind to eliminate random thoughts when desired, and thus become a more enjoyable and useful servant to you.

Chapter Twenty Two
Be Master of Yourself

To be the master of your emotions, your ego and your rational mind is one of the greatest things you or any human being can do. It may be beautiful to paint pictures, build buildings or write great novels. But to become the master of yourself is an even higher accomplishment to mankind — and to yourself.

To stay on the pathway to higher consciousness, it may help to recall three factors that represent consciousness growth. They are so closely related that an advancement in any one of the three will cause an advancement in the other two. They are:

1.) Eliminate your addictions.
2.) Quiet your rational mind.
3.) Disidentify with the "self" which your ego guards so constantly.

The first two factors have already been covered, so we will go on to the third. As children we learn to experience territory as "myself" or "mine" and we generate the experience of irritation or anger when people appear to encroach on territory we consider our own. Since the ego is constantly busy protecting the territory it has defined as "mine" it can never relax and enjoy the here and now. It must always be securing its future happiness. The frequency with which one's biocomputer runs off addictive programming creates the illusion that the "I" or "self" is an entity — a "somebody" — rather than a robot-like activity.

When the activity of "self" is recognized as an activity, rather than as an entity, we begin to see that we are responsible for our suffering. The "I" is this activity of defense. When we stop defending, there is no more "I" or "self." With each addiction that you are successful in reducing to a preference, you will find that a bit of this "self" disappears. Instead of experiencing people as objects, you increasingly feel them as "us" or "like me." Gradually this sharply-defined experience of "self" leaves you. You then begin to identify with other people, even when they do something that previously would have triggered an angry response in you. You just see that they are doing what you have done many times, and you do not throw them out of your heart.

You can recognize most addictions by the awareness that your biocomputer is programming feelings of negativity — fear, anger, irritation, boredom etc. The more subtle ones may be harder to recognize, such as preoccupation and inability to concentrate on a problem. As your consciousness gains relative freedom from being dominated by your addictions, you will intuitively find the answers to problems, and you will find that "thinking" (juggling words, hypotheses and ideas around a problem) is usually not the way to find the optimal solution. A free, undominated awareness that is highly tuned to the here and now, the people and situations around you, will best enable you to benefit by the wisdom that is waiting to be tapped in your biocomputer. Your problem is to get at the wisdom that you already have — but which is inaccessible to you now because of your security, sensation and power-dominated consciousness.

The level of consciousness at which you operate determines what you notice and what you don't notice. Your programming influences whether you see it all clearly, or see it through distorting ego filters — whether it grabs your consciousness or is simply seen for what it is. Love and peace are not only your goals, they are also the methods you use to get to the goals. Always realize that it is only the programming in your head that is separating you from the beautiful feelings of higher consciousness every second of your life. Happiness is here waiting inside of you — and it becomes more available everytime you reprogram one of your addictions.

The Brotherhoods say that if the quest for attainment of Egoic advancement could be put into one word, that word would be "awareness" (*The Ultimate Frontier*, p. 173). In order to have awareness, we must have knowledge and experience. We need to have awareness of ourselves, our environment and of the universe. We need to know how our body and mind function, and how other people react to us, and we to them, so that we can all work toward eventual oneness with all mankind. In order to get a better understanding of our mind, we will go into more detail here on its construction and operation.

The brain, or biocomputer, is unbelievably complex. The eye alone has over two million nerve fibers connecting it to the brain. The ear has about two hundred thousand. Every hair on our bodies is connected to the brain by a nerve fiber. Our skin, our internal organs, and other parts of the body further complicate the network of the nervous system. Most of this information sent to the brain is on the unconscious level. It is filtered and re-filtered, abstracted and re-abstracted, and routed to the proper brain center, either conscious or subconscious. Perhaps only one-millionth part of the impulses received by the brain are on the conscious level. Naturally the rest of the impulses, which is almost all of them, we are not conscious of, so some aspects must be left out each time there is an abstraction. (The verb "abstract" in this sense means "to reduce to a summary.") For instance, a smooth table top is not really smooth — it is composed of atoms and molecules, which in turn are composed of sub-atomic particles whirling around in their individual orbits. Our senses do not permit us to tune in to reality — they only pick up that small portion that is transmittable through electromagnetic impulses.

Further, the brain manufactures, manipulates, distorts and changes the received impulses according to memory, addictions, experience and personality. An example of this is that when listening to a small portable radio, we hear sounds that are not actually there, such as the bass notes of music, which the small radio speaker is incapable of reproducing, but which is supplied to some extent by our own auditory system. The brain can tell they belong there, and it supplies them.

The cerebral cortex is a thin outer covering of the sides and upper parts of the convoluted surfaces of the brain, which has from ten to thirteen billion cortical cells. These brain cells and their connections are the structures that enable our rational mind to be aware of being aware, to use words and symbols, and to comprehend complex systems of thought, such as mathematics, science and art. Although we possess this magnificent equipment, we are not automatically expert in knowing how to use it. The activity of the brain can be measured by the electro-encephalograph, that detects alpha waves and beta waves. The subject-object activities of the first three centers of consciousness generally produce beta waves. As we go into the fourth and fifth centers of consciousness, our cerebral cortex begins to produce more alpha waves.

One of the underlying processing systems of the brain is the limbic system, that plays a paramount part in the generation of emotional feelings. One of its major functions is to compare the incoming stimuli of the body and the sensory receptors with the programmed instructions that have been put into it by our experiences to date. The limbic system interacts with the cerebral cortex for analyzing such data. The hippocampus, which is part of the limbic system, plays a part in evaluating the incoming stimuli in terms of one's past experience.

The amygdala, another component of the limbic system, functions to intensify an emotional response whenever anything new and unexpected happens. It will send out impulses of emotional reaction which travel through the thalamic area and trigger the release of hormones that cause you to feel upset, increase the adrenalin in your blood, speed up your heart rate, increase your blood sugar, and do other things to prepare you for a "fight or flight" reaction.

Another part of the limbic system is the septal region, which plays a role in toning down our emotional reactions. The activation of this system helps to release us from emotional tension.

Still another vital part of the brain is the reticular activity system (RAS). It is a cone-shaped complex of nerves radiating from the brain stem. It functions as the "door keeper" to our consciousness, determining what to allow to go through. It can put you to sleep or wake you up. If you are deeply occupied, it can shut off incoming stimuli so that you can concentrate. However, your RAS is programmed to override your concentration in certain cases, such as when someone enters the room. Your RAS interacting with your programming determines what you perceive. You do not see the world as it is — you over-emphasize the small slice of world that resonates with your fears, demands, hopes and expectations. As you grow into higher consciousness your RAS will react to love and acceptance programming, and then your love will create your world.

You should keep your aims realistic, and enjoy taking one step at a time. Once the major part of your consciousness resides in the love center, you will experience a happiness and beauty in your life that is "enough." Even if you do not progress beyond this center, you will have a wisdom and effectiveness in your life that will exceed that of most of the people in the world. Enjoy the eternally beautiful here and now moment that your life continually offers you. At the end of your journey toward awakening you will find your real self.

The following is reprinted from an article in Parade Magazine of August 6, 1978, and illustrates how many intelligent men arrive at the same conclusions about life independently and in their own ways. The article was written by Pam Proctor.

After spending a lifetime studying and writing about men and events, historian-philosopher Will Durant, 92, has distilled more than 2,000 years of history into three simple words, "love one another."

"My final lesson of history," says Durant, "is the same as that of Jesus."

"You may think that's a lot of lollipop," Durant adds with a laugh. "But just try it. Love is the most practical thing in the world."

History has taught Durant to be "realistic" about human nature. "I accept man as history shows him to be: good and bad, competitive and cooperative. The best I can do is take human beings as they are and assume that they are going to be decent. And I find that if I make that assumption, it helps them to be decent.

"If you take an attitude of love toward everybody you meet, you'll eventually get along."

These are paradoxical words from a man who turned his back on the Roman Catholic priesthood and the church nearly three quarters of a century ago to seek his salvation in the study of philosophy and history. In 1926 he published the best-selling book The Story of Philosophy, which gave him the financial means to embark on his monumental 11-volume series The Story of Civilization. The last five volumes were co-authored by his wife of 64 years, Ariel. One of the books, Rousseau and Revolution, published when he was 82 and she 69, won them the Pulitzer Prize.

The Durants approached each period of history by asking the question: "Who were the people in this age still influential on human life?"

"In any generation," says Durant, "there may be eight or ten persons who will be alive in the sense of continuing influence 300 years after. For instance, Plato still is. Socrates still is." But in all of Western civilization, the person who stands out above all others, says Durant, is Christ. "He was undoubtedly the most permanent influence on our thoughts, but not on our actions. And that is an important modification.

"Our actions are very seldom Christian. But our theology often is. We wish we could behave like Christ."

Durant adds, "The most essential thing I see in the universe is creative power." He sees it "in all fields — not only in woman bearing the child, which is the fundamental form of human creation, but in the man thinking, the woman thinking, the mathematician discovering new formulas. There is creation going on all the time; the child taking pleasure in jumping, the boy looking at the girl with wonder, and the man looking at the woman with desire."

In ending the interview, Durant quoted Socrates: "Life without an attempt to understand it is hardly worth living."

Chapter Twenty Three
Practicing the Virtues

We have gone on at some length about the higher centers of consciousness described in *The Handbook to Higher Consciousness*, but we have only briefly mentioned the Twelve Great Virtues of the Brotherhoods. In this chapter a description will be given of these Virtues, so that they will not be just words with vague meanings and soon forgotten.

I believe it is most important to develop a positive attitude and cheerful outlook toward life. The Love and Cornucopia Centers of consciousness, if we eliminate our addictions, will give us loving acceptance of others; the Conscious-Awareness Center will help us in reprogramming to eliminate the "self" concept; and practicing the Great Virtues will aid us in building character, and thus create greater happiness for ourselves and for others in our lives. All these things work together and overlap one another. After we have learned and applied the suggestions, and are operating on the Love Center of consciousness, the Virtues will fall naturally into our expanding consciousness. But, as in everything else, we must be aware of them in order to make the best use of them. As mentioned earlier, practice of the Virtues is one of the requirements for initiation into the Brotherhoods.

Tolerance is the wisdom of not making judgments on our fellow men, since we can never be sure of their true motivations, trials and personal problems. Criticism of others' beliefs, habits and personalities is unwarranted, self-righteous and inexcusable. The tolerant man does not measure others only by their errors, but rather he asks himself how he would have reacted under identical circumstances. In place of a critical, irritable attitude toward another, which can only add to the cross he must bear, the tolerant man is slow to speak and act, lest he detract from his opportunity to spread happiness and peace into the lives of those with whom he comes in contact. To detract from the reputation of another by gossip and hearsay is karmically disastrous.

Patience is the willingness to await the outworking of natural processes. Patience stresses calmness or composure under suffering or provocation or in performing a demanding task. Impatience with another person arises from lack of tolerance and a selfish peevishness to have one's own way. To fail to take the time to explain to a child or an employee what was to be done and then jump down his throat because the task was not performed as desired, is a typical example of impatience. Impatience is a major source of irritability in the world, and much of this is due to desires which cannot be realized realistically.

Kindliness is the sincere desire never to bring hurt to another. It is consideration of the feelings of others as well as gentleness, sensitivity, benevolence and sympathy expressed in word and deed.

Forbearance is self-possession and serenity of mind under any provocation, and conveys the patient lack of a desire for retaliation. It is the overcoming of revengeful reaction to personal affronts and injuries. The nursing of grudges only breeds bitterness and psychosomatic illness. Forbearance is an attitude of non-resistance and a bending with the situation. Knowledge of karmic law provides the comfort that one's retaliation against an offender is pointless in light of the natural law of action and reaction. The offender will suffer karmically without us engaging in destructive thoughts; thus forbearance breaks the circle of repercussions typical of feuds. Forbearance becomes an exercise in humility; for personal pride and the need to uphold self are common causes of retaliatory instincts.

Charity stresses brotherly love, clemency, leniency and an interest in the welfare of others to the extent of giving of oneself. It is whole-hearted sympathy for the suffering which man must endure until he begins conscious advancement. Charity precludes criticism of others.

Humility connotes absence of arrogance, snobbishness, pride, boastfulness and self-satisfaction. Humility does not imply weakness; rather it is the result of strength, power and true personal completeness so that one need not feel he must contend for a place in the sun. Similarly, meekness is the absence of wrath, and it stems from a sense of complete control over one's environment. Humility is the awareness of one's own shortcomings in view of the knowledge that Virtue always recedes from one's present standing and that one has far to go to achieve even the first degree of Brotherhood.

Devotion is the consecration of oneself to an ideal or a cause, such as to the service of God. Devotion implies singleness of purpose which supplies an interest so great that serving the object of one's devotion is a joyful, untiring experience. The finer emotions of allegiance, faithfulness, loyalty, steadfastness and reverence are involved in devotion, but to this is added zeal of service due to love of, and personal attachment to, the object of devotion.

Sincerity conveys the absence of hypocrisy, affectatiousness, sham or deceit. The sincere person is genuine and straight forward in his desire to learn and practice what is right. Conscientiousness and honorable conduct are closely associated with sincerity; but sincerity should be practiced with knowledge of right thought and actions because most of the evil and wrongheaded errors brought upon the world have been the result of sincere though misinformed persons. The acquisition of the other Virtues is impossible without sincerity, and the depth of application it affords.

Courage is quite distinct from bravery, which is usually an instinctual response to a perilous situation, and implies lack of fear and bold recklessness. Courage, on the other hand, carefully takes into account the dangers of a situation in advance of action and is the product of reason sustained by marshaling one's powers of moral determination in the face of personal fear. Resolution, tenacity and determined morale are associated with courage; and it is the noble quality of character that enables one to stand firmly for his convictions in spite of persecution.

Precision involves exactness, accuracy and definiteness, as opposed to purposeless activity, careless work and hazy thinking. Forethought, dependability, punctuality and thoroughness are hallmarks of the precise person. To remain a virtue, however, precision must not become piddling fussiness, or a display of meticulousness which intolerably compares those of lesser preciseness and strips away all beauty from every situation in order to exhibit precision.

Efficiency is the ability to deal effectively with one's environment with a minimum expenditure of energy, time and materials. To become more efficient requires an alert interest in methods and techniques and the acquisition of skills through practice. Attention to organization of details and planning ahead are the mark of an efficient person. Precision is inseparable from efficiency.

Discrimination implies the power of discerning the motives of people and their character, and the ability to see the real truths below the apparent surface of situations. To discriminate emphasizes the power to distinguish the excellent and the appropriate; to judge between what is good and what is better; to weigh alternative action in the light of karmic law; and to perceive the fallaciousness of teachings that are disseminated under the guise of all that is good and beautiful. Intuition is a natural extension of the power of discrimination.

(Reprinted from "Observations" by Richard Kieninger, *The Lemurian Builder*, Vol. 3, no. 2, Feb. 1968.)

In order to become familiar with the Virtues, try taking one each week and carrying it with you in your head while at your daily routine. At the end of the day, think back on your performance of that virtue during the situations in which you were involved, and grade yourself plus or minus for each situation. In this way you will soon discover which virtues need the most improvement in your life.

Acquiring the Great Virtues is a slow process, but a very rewarding one, both in greater awareness and happiness for yourself, and in the powerful positive energy you generate in all others with whom you come in contact. With the application of the Virtues to your life, in conjunction with the points already studied, and the living love method to rid yourself of your addictions, you should be well on your way along the pathway to higher consciousness. Remember, *we are perfect beings;* have always been and will always be perfect. It is only what is in our heads, our thoughts, that make us imperfect. With this knowledge you can throw out all negative thoughts and become a joyous, loving entity.

Chapter Twenty Four
Selecting a Suitable Environment

In order to attain rapid Egoic development, it helps to have a favorable environment in which to live, work and play, so that our bodies and minds have an opportunity to take advantage of the situations and circumstances placed in our paths, and use them for expanding our consciousness.

The community of Stelle, in Stelle, Illinois, was organized for this very purpose, and at this writing is in full operation, with most of the amenities for comfortable living and quiet surroundings, in order for the members of the Stelle Group to be able to study, work, rear and educate their children, and live a full life while advancing rapidly to Initiate in the Brotherhoods, with eventual progress to Mastership.

It is not possible, nor would it be desirable, for everyone who reads this book to join the Stelle Group and move to the City of Stelle, but it is possible for anyone to improve his environment, if he has a genuine desire to do so. A great many people who live in crowded cities full of noise, pollution, impure air, crime and violence and other hazards of city life would like to get out of the city and move to rural areas. But most of them do nothing about it, because they are tied down to a job, friends or relatives, or have become stuck in a rut that has developed into an addiction so that they believe they cannot escape. Others do break away, some to weekend places and some to new permanent homes. Some find peace and happiness in these moves, and some find only more drudgery and hard work in rushing away to a weekend place, doing all the necessary chores to make and keep it livable, then rushing back to home and work again. I am speaking from experience now, because my wife and I did this for many years before finally moving out of the metropolitan area where we lived, and starting anew in the country near a small town. We found this to be very satisfying, and we are still here after 20 years.

There are some people who are so city-bred that they actually need the noise of traffic and the other noises of the city in order to be comfortable, and when they come to visit us in the country, they can't sleep because it is too quiet. But these noises are definitely harmful to our physical well-being, and this has been proven by statistics. This is true as well with the sounds of radio or television constantly blaring their brainwashing advertising and other drivel of soap operas, game shows, situation comedies with dubbed-in laughter, and so on ad infinitum.

There is one good thing about radio and TV, however — they can be turned off. The only way to get rid of city noises, jet planes near airports, and other objectionable sounds is to move away from them. There are many, many places where the air is still pure, nature is still relatively unspoiled and the sounds one hears are mostly of quail, an occasional blue jay, and various other bird and animal life, or perhaps a raccoon at night trying to get into the garbage can. We live in such a place, and we are thankful to be here. But some day we will have a problem, when we are no longer able to drive a car. Then we will have to find another place within walking distance to shopping. That is a point to consider when selecting a place, if one is getting close to that stage in life.

People also have different likes and dislikes, depending on where they spent their early years, their temperaments and present environments. Some can stand extremes of temperature very well. Others can't. If one can afford it, it would be nice to spend the summers in the north and winters in the south. And it is not so impossible as it may sound. I know of one couple who are not wealthy or well-to-do by any means, yet manage to spend their winters on the beach at Mazatlan, Mexico, and their summers at home in California. The thing to remember is that you can do almost anything if you set your mind to it, and figure out a way to make it work. Your concentration and desire will help you in bringing other favorable influences and conditions to you to help in furthering your plan. When you do this, you are precipitating the thing you desire, and the stronger your thoughts are, the more energy in thought form you radiate, and the more likely you will be to precipitate favorable conditions for the success of your venture. Think only positively, never negatively or doubtfully.

If you would like to improve your environment, but don't have any particular place in mind to "get away from it all," a good way to start looking is to travel around to likely spots on your vacation. We started out years ago with a tent, progressed to a small trailer, then a larger one, and finally a camper van, which we now have, and like it best because of its easy handling, comfort and convenience and reasonably good fuel mileage. Of course, one can fly or take the bus, but I prefer to have my own transportation handy at all times, in order to explore and enjoy all the places that are accessible only by car, such as the state and national parks, the mountains and seashore, lakes and streams, towns and villages.

The area of the country with which I am most familiar is the Pacific Coast, so I will describe a few spots that I believe would be good locations for a person or family that is searching for peaceful living and happiness. Starting at the Canadian border and working south, I heard recently of an area in Washington that has an exceptionally fine climate, although it is located farther north than the state of

Maine. It is on the east side of the Olympic Peninsula, which is the part of Washington that is bounded by Puget Sound on the east, the Strait of Juan de Fuca on the north, and the Pacific Ocean on the west. On the western slopes of the Olympic Mountains on the peninsula, it rains as much as 150 inches a year average rainfall, but on the eastern slopes and in the valley beyond, it rains as little as 16 inches a year. This valley is called the Dungeness Valley, between Port Townsend and Port Angeles. It is a popular area for retired people, and all the facilities for modern living are there. The town of Sequim (pronounced Skwim) is right in the middle of the valley, and the Chamber of Commerce there supplied us with information about the climate, housing and other things we wanted to know.

All of western Washington is beautiful and green, but the climate is more severe in some parts.

Whidbey Island, in Puget Sound, is in the same general "sun belt" location as Dungeness Valley, and also has a mild and relatively dry climate. It is the second largest island in the country, so I am told, and has only two towns of importance. It is reached from Port Townsend by ferry, or by a bridge at the north end of the island, from Mt. Vernon. From Port Angeles, which is about 15 miles west of Sequim, a ferry will take you across the Strait to Victoria, B.C., a delightful city to visit. This is all boating country, and if you are a boating fan, you will probably like it here.

Highway 101 crosses the Columbia River on a 4½-mile long bridge into Oregon, and follows the coastline most of the way south to California. It is a rugged, rocky coast, with big rocks scattered along offshore, and wide flat beaches. There are several rivers emptying into the ocean from the Coast Range Mountains farther inland. Any of this territory would be a good choice for a quiet, peaceful existence, if you don't mind a lot of rain. Rainfall figures run around 40 to 60 inches annually, but this keeps the country green and beautiful, and the weather is usually sunny and mild between rains.

Farther inland, in the Willamette Valley and south to the California border, are also mostly green meadows and some forest land on the Coast Range and in the Cascade Mountains. It is all fine country, depending on your preferences. On the east slope of the Cascades, in the area around Bend, are many lakes and ponderosa pine forests, with some snow in the winter and rather warm temperatures in summer. Further south is the Klamath Falls, Crater Lake and Rogue River country. The Rogue is noted for its salmon fishing, all the way from Grants Pass to the mouth at Gold Beach. It also has gorgeous scenery and is a favorite vacation spot, drawing many people each year to "run the rapids."

Not far south in California, the areas around Mt. Shasta and Mt. Lassen are attractions for retired persons seeking homes. East of Mt. Lassen the High Sierra country begins, and there is Susanville and other towns and many mountain lakes and streams. Continuing south, we come to Lake Tahoe, and over to the west, Clear Lake, both of which are fine places to live. The Sierras also have many more attractive locations, and a ride along the foothills on Highway 49 will give you an idea of what living is like among the people in the various old gold-rush towns of the area.

About 60 miles north of San Francisco is the Russian River, a really wonderful expanse of redwood forests, meadows and vineyards, and to the east is Napa Valley, another beautiful vineyard country, from Napa north to St. Helena and Calistoga.

South of San Francisco, the Santa Cruz mountains and Monterey Bay are noteworthy. Santa Barbara is a "horsey" community, with Spanish architecture, on a bay of the Pacific Ocean. From here south to Mexico the coast is mostly too heavily populated to be attractive, but farther inland on Highway 395 is desert that many people like. I like the desert in the spring and fall months of the year, when the temperature is moderate.

Going south on 395 you come to a pretty little valley, and the city of Escondido, in a setting of avocado and orange groves. It and other towns nearby have a very good climate, pleasant surroundings, and are close, but not too close, to San Diego, the Mexican border, Salton Sea, Mt. Palomar, Borrega State Park and other attractions.

These are by no means all of the places you could find in the Pacific Coast area to live in quiet and serenity, and I am sure that in the other 47 states there are plenty of other beautiful spots for working toward higher consciousness.

Chapter Twenty Five
What is Reality?

In this materialistic age, we have been trained to believe that the only reality is the physical one, which we can perceive with our five senses. The spiritual existence, which some of us can feel in varying degree, is something that has not been investigated scientifically to a great extent. And research into the workings of the mind is still in its infancy. But men are constantly investigating, probing and experimenting in the various fields of science, medicine, philosophy, psychology, parapsychology and the occult sciences, as well as digging into ancient knowledge of history, religion, and science. They are finding out more and more to indicate that there are other planes of existence, or realities. The Brotherhoods say there are seven, and each has its own reality. There may be other realities, too, such as those we experience when we are in a dream state, or in other levels of consciousness. And since time and space have entirely different values in all planes other than the Physical, we should consider the realities of the past and future as well as of the present. And perhaps there are more realities that we simply cannot comprehend with our limited minds and senses, that are in an entirely different dimension. And again, reality is not the same to everyone, because each of us sees, feels, hears, smells and touches according to his own beliefs rather than according to the facts. As one's mind and experiences develop during the normal living process, his ideas of reality also change.

All this becomes very confusing, but it is necessary for us to be aware of reality in order to deal with it successfully. I think we just have to go along with it, learn as much as we can about it, and trust God to guide us in learning more as we progress, when we are ready for it. Our first task is to learn all we can about life on the Physical Plane — for instance, to become aware of the beauties of nature, to recognize the good in people and to love them unconditionally, to love animals and be kind to them, to develop our spiritual selves and our mental capacities, to take care of our physical bodies in order to surmount life's obstacles. When we have done all these things, we have built up our character in the process, and increased our awareness of reality.

The reality of immortality has intrigued thinking men throughout the ages, and I have taken excerpts from an article in the magazine Modern Maturity to quote the thoughts and beliefs of great men on this subject.*

Cicero: There is in the minds of men, I know not how, a certain presage, as it were, of a future existence, and this takes root most deeply in the greatest geniuses and most exalted souls.

Ralph Waldo Emerson: Where man ripens, this belief (in immortality) presently appears. As soon as thought is exercised, this belief is inevitable.

Spinoza (eminent philosopher): We feel and experience ourselves to be immortal.

Pascal (philosopher-physicist): Is it more difficult to return to being than to come into it?

Darwin: To those who fully admit to immortality of the human soul, the destruction of our world will not appear so dreadful.

---

*Reprinted with permission from Modern Maturity, copyright 1978 by the American Association of Retired Persons.

William Faulkner (Nobel Prize-winning author): I believe that man will not only endure, he will prevail. I believe man is immortal because he has a soul, a spirit capable of compassion and sacrifice, and endurance.

Edwin Markham (noted poet): Life is but the stuff to try the soul on.

Thomas A. Edison, when he was dying: It is very beautiful over there.

Beethoven believed his deafness would be restored when he left this world.

Albert Schweitzer: Let a man begin to think about the mystery of his life and the links that connect his with the life that fills the world, and he cannot but bring to bear on his own life and all others that come within his reach the principle of reverence for life, and manifest this principle by ethical affirmation of life.

Senator Everett Dirksen: Man will live again as surely as day follows night.

Arthur H. Compton (Nobel Prize-winning physicist): It takes a whole lifetime to build the character of a noble man. The adventures and disciplines of youth, the struggles and failures and successes, the pain and pleasure of maturity, the loneliness and tranquility of age — these make up the fire through which he must pass to bring out the pure gold of his soul. Having been thus perfected, what shall nature do with him? Annihilate him? What infinite waste! I prefer to believe he lives on after death, continuing in a larger sphere, in cooperation with his Maker, the work he has begun.

Norman Vincent Peale: Careful experiments approved by competent mathematicians seem to indicate that there is another aspect of man besides the physical, not governed by space or time.

Hornell Hart (professor at Duke University and lifetime researcher in psychic and ESP phenomena): Over three million tests have demonstrated that the mind of man can function independently of time and space, as we understand them. To me this is proof that the soul transcends the body. The spiritual version of reality is now the one that is supported by the evidence. Our true existence is beyond both space and time. And the event called death in our earthly lives can be but an episode in the far vaster adventure.

Victor Hugo: I feel immortality within myself. The nearer I approach to the end, the more plainly I hear the immortal symphonies of the world to come.

This is only a small sampling. Among others who expressed similar thoughts are Socrates, Plato, Kant, Goethe, Henry James, Robert Milliken, and Albert Einstein.

These men did not allow the spiritual aspect of their lives to become completely submerged in the turbulent sea of practical living. When one takes time to sit quietly and cleanse his thoughts of mundane matters of everyday living, he can begin to think more clearly and become aware within himself of the feelings of a spiritual nature that are ordinarily suppressed. If we could but relax and maintain a calm serenity while grappling with life's problems, how much better we could handle them! This is the reason that meditation is so valuable, and the reason it is being practiced by so many business people today.

Every race, every religion, every cult has different ideas about what the true reality is. The Yogi, for example, believes that physical existence is only an illusion, and that reality exists only after one's mind is absorbed into the one Universal Mind. He seeks to achieve this goal by performing the various physical and mental exercises taught by the Yoga philosophy. The philosopher Spinoza expounded a theory of reality quite similar in many ways to that of the Brotherhoods. To me, the philosophy of the Brotherhoods is the only one that can withstand the tests and conditions by which all others fail.

Chapter Twenty Six
Learning to Love

When we said earlier that in order to raise ourselves above the lower consciousness levels of security, sensation and power, we must learn to love everyone unconditionally, including ourselves, it was a pretty big bite to chew all at once. We have been so conditioned otherwise by the lifestyle we follow, and the ingrained instincts of competition and survival, that it is going to take a lot of doing to reverse these thoughts that keep popping up in every situation.

Since, in the final analysis, we are all children struggling along the road to Egoic advancement, why not take a look at children and see if they can teach us something about love. I am far from being an expert on children, not having had any of our own, but we did have a foster child living with us for several years, and nieces and nephews galore. I also taught a 4-H class for a year, and learned something from each of these experiences. I think children do have a message for us if we are able to recognize and comprehend it. It is the same old refrain we have heard before: "love everyone unconditionally." Look into the eyes of a small child, and notice the love, trust and faith displayed there. They know instinctively the oneness of all people, until they learn later on that the ideal conditions they assume are not actually true, because, and only because, of the thoughts and actions of the people around them. Children need unconditional love, and they want to give unconditional love, and the more they get the more they have to give. Do you remember your childhood days, when you fully expected your mother and father to be absolutely perfect and to do no wrong? Then later on you may have discovered they had feet of clay like everyone else, and this was a big let-down, but also necessary as part of your learning process. I don't think you loved your parents any less than before, but perhaps with a little more compassion for their weaknesses. Now you can realize that they were just playing out their dramas and sufferings in their struggle on the path to higher consciousness, like all the rest of us.

The Christian Children's Fund, of Richmond, Virginia, is a charitable organization founded on a small scale about forty years ago in China, and which now has grown until it has branches all over the world. It helps children of all races and creeds with food, shelter, clothing and schooling, through sponsorship by interested persons at $18 per month per child. I joined this group a year ago, with some doubts, but all those doubts have long since been dispelled, and the whole experience has been very happy and rewarding, with the best yet to come when I am finally able to visit my two sponsored children, one in Mexico and the other in Brazil. Their whole operation is built on love — you can tell it in every aspect of the enterprise, especially in the children's letters, the attitudes of the people working with the children and in the offices, and the letters published in the CCF magazine from grateful sponsors who have found new outlets for their love. I believe there are other organizations similar to this one, doing as fine or possibly even finer work, but there can never be enough to care for the millions of starving, sick and homeless children in the world. There are plenty of them right here in the United States, but at least our government has some programs to help deal with this condition. The CCF has a program going for American Indian children here. The Bureau of Indian Affairs has been

Learning to Love

criticized in the past for its policies; whether rightly so or not, I don't know. In addition to these children there are the Blacks, Mexicans, Puerto Ricans and migrant workers' groups, all needing help and love. Why is love so important in our lives? Because it elevates the spirit to a higher vibratory level, raising us for the moment, above the lower consciousness levels of security, sensation and power. When we are operating on the love level of consciousness, we can achieve happiness, peace and serenity, which we can never achieve on the lower consciousness levels. In fact, love is the greatest thing in the world. That is a broad statement, but many men believe it is so, and the Bible also says it is so. Quoting Paul, "If I have all faith so that I can remove mountains, and have not love, I am nothing." And John said, "God *is* love." When you have love in your heart, you are close to oneness with God. We said love is the greatest thing in the world. But love is not a thing at all; it is a combination, like a chemical compound, of all the virtues which we know and try to live by. If one follows the Twelve Great Virtues of the Brotherhoods, he is bound to acquire love along with them. The poet Browning wrote this about love:

> *"Love, I say, is energy of life.*
> *For life, with all it yields of joy or woe*
> *And hope and fear,*
> *Is just our chance o' the prize of learning*
> *Love, —*
> *How love might be, hath been indeed,*
> *   and is."*

We pass through this life but once. If we ignore the opportunities to give of ourselves to others, or commit the sins of omission, we lose the chance to uplift our character which was placed in our path. We should train ourselves to look upon every situation and circumstance as a new challenge for our Egoic advancement.

In learning to love, we must unlearn some things. One of the most important of these is anger or bad temper. When anger flares up, love goes out the window. Anger can be called the vice of the virtuous. It is one of the most destructive forces in our world, and should be curbed at all costs. Again quoting from the Bible, Christ said, "I say unto you, that the publicans and the harlots go into the Kingdom of God before you." There is no place in Heaven for anger or ill-temper. To enter Heaven, a man must take it with him. Temper is a significant trait not in what it is alone, but in what it reveals. It is a test for love, a symptom, a revelation of an unloving nature within. For a lack of patience, a lack of kindness, a lack of generosity, courtesy and unselfishness are all instantaneously symbolized in a flash of temper.

So it is not enough to deal with the temper. We must go to the source and change the innermost nature. Then the angry humors will die away. Souls are made sweet not by taking the acids out, but by putting something in — a great love. Then, and only then, can the angry person achieve inner peace and happiness. I was quick-tempered when I was young, and had to learn the hard way how to control it and finally eliminate it, so I know it can be done. But I am still working on it, to reprogram my mind for love rather than anger. It makes life so much more fun! But life is not a playground, it is a school. It is not a holiday, but an education. And the one eternal lesson for us all is: how better we can love. When we do this, we build up our character and our knowledge and experience, and make great strides forward on our pathway to advancement.

At the risk of repeating myself in the next few paragraphs, let me emphasize that learning to love better is like doing physical exercise or learning a language. It takes constant practice, and that is what we are here for. In order to practice, we must get into the mainstream of life where there are other people and situations with whom we can interact and allow our love to flow out to them, and theirs to come to us.

We cannot command love to enter our Souls, for love is an effect, and to gain this effect there must be a cause. The cause must originate with us, if it is to have an effect on us. We must have love for Christ and His laws before we can acquire the effect. But Christ said that you do not need all the other laws laid down by the Ten Commandments and later elaborated on, if you have love. It takes care of all the other laws. So, by accepting and loving Christ, we have initiated the cause, and the effect will follow.

Another reason that love is the greatest thing in the world, is that it is permanent; it lasts; it is eternal. Nothing physical in our world is permanent. The Earth itself will some day be gone — but love is everlasting, like our Egos or Souls, and love is the only one of the things we have collected here that we can take with us when it is time to leave. Faith and hope are also everlasting, but they are only a part of love.

To those who are looking for answers to such questions as: What is in store for me? How can I help myself to find a better life and a better hereafter? The key word is love. Paraphrasing John Kennedy, "It's not what God is doing for you, but what are you doing for God?" Ask yourself these questions: Have I helped others in need? Have I been kind and thoughtful and unselfish to others? Have I refrained from criticism and judgment of others? Have I practiced all the virtues to the best of my ability? If your answers are "No," you probably do not have love in your heart, and probably are not living a fulfilling, happy life. It is easy to change this — just open your heart and let the love flow out — and in.

God *is* love. Christ said so.

Love is the greatest thing in the world.

To order additional copies of LIFE AND LOVE, please write:

                Ray Garfield
                P.O. Box 4125
                Clearlake, CA 95422

Please send $5.95 per copy (postpaid). California residents add 6 percent sales tax.